Hansi's
New Life

Hansi's New Life

MARIA ANNE HIRSCHMANN

FLEMING H. REVELL COMPANY
Old Tappan, New Jersey

All Scripture references in this book are based on the King James Version of the Bible.

Library of Congress Cataloging in Publication Data

Hirschmann, Maria Anne.
    Hansi's new life.

    1. Hirschmann, Maria Anne. I. Title.
BX6193.H54A29   973.92'092'4 [B]   75–11561
ISBN 0–8007–0740–0

TO the new generation of America
and to my children. . . .
May they not only be Americans by birth,
but by their free choice and
God's special calling.

Contents

Foreword

Europeans sometimes see America differently from the Americans themselves. It is interesting to read in this book what an immigrant from Czechoslovakia saw, heard, and experienced in this country.

More important is it that we learn from this book what it means to receive forgiveness from God and how to forgive others. When Hansi tells about my forgiving the Germans, she shows what Jesus Christ is willing to give out of His glorious, unlimited resources—the mighty inner strengthening of His Holy Spirit (*see* Ephesians 3:16).

What we are not able to do, Jesus can, and He is willing to teach us when we obey Him. What a joy that He never lets you down.

Jesus is Victor.

CORRIE TEN BOOM

Retrace

It was a nightmare. It had to be. I would wake up shortly to my normal life. Though filled with hardships, this life held out high hopes, idealism—proud words declared the certainty of future victory. I could hardly wait for the announcement that would broadcast to the world that our Nazi Germany had triumphed over her enemies.

But—that nightmare! I never realized that a person could, simultaneously, have so many hideous dreams and feel it was reality.

A radio blared out that *Hitler was dead.* Ridiculous. Hitler couldn't be dead. The war was not yet over and he had promised us—the German people—that he would lead our nation to ultimate victory. And, anyway, wasn't Hitler a god? The god I worshiped! Gods do not die. It *must* be all a dream.

Another part of the dream was that the Russians were in our city: plundering, raping, terrorizing, and killing the German people at will. But how was that possible?

We Germans had been sovereign in my homeland, Czechoslovakia, since, in 1938, Nazi troops occupied the land and made it a German protectorate. And why should we not have this right to conquer? Were not we Germans the superrace called by the Supreme Power of the Universe to bring about a better way of life to peoples of the world? In my young idealistic heart I could never understand why almost everyone seemed so determined to hate us and battle us for this ideal. World War II had been raging for five years. Surely it was time to bring that madness to an end; we must get on with teaching the glory of Nazism all over the globe!

My dream reverie ended abruptly, broken by the trembling voice of my older sister saying, "Well, the war is finally over—but what will happen to all of us now?" Her words were dreadfully real. I shook myself awake, a choking sensation in my throat. I blinked into the glaring sunlight and my brain began hammering it in: "You're not dreaming; you're awake."

My nightmare was reality. *Germany had lost the war!* Hitler was dead—and all was lost. It had never dawned on me, even to the last, that such a thing could possibly happen. When it did, it hit me so hard that my mind refused to register the truth of it, in the way that a computer rejects false input. I felt myself falling—falling into a deep, dark pit of confusion. After seemingly endless falling, I hit bottom and lay there shattered into a thousand pieces. Nothing made sense! Life had no more meaning. Neither did death. *Maybe, I thought, it would be best to follow Hitler's example and die by suicide. Could that be the only way out? Oh, for someone who would tell me what to do!* I wasn't used to making decisions for myself anymore. All my life I had been taught that unquestioning obedience was what I needed most to learn. Having arrived there, to everyone's satisfaction, I now found myself helpless. I knew not in which direction to go, whose orders to follow.

I found myself pondering: *Why was life so terribly cruel?* From the beginning, mine had never been an easy life. Born into poverty and orphaned as a baby, I was kept for God's and for pity's sake, by a humble Christian family. Food was never plentiful during my childhood. Neither was outward display of love. The struggle for survival had marked the people of my Sudeten Mountains deeply, for the soil was barren and the winters hard and I learned very early in life to fight—fight to stay alive.

My foster-father had a deep conviction that bulls and children needed to have their wills broken while young. Since we were too poor to ever own a bull, he tried his best to break *my* will.

I think a bull could have been more easily subdued than I! Poor Father! How I poisoned his life with my wordless stubbornness. Not that I didn't try to be obedient. I wanted to, but my spirit did not seem to be able to yield to his authority and orders *without questioning.* That ability I finally acquired while in Nazi school.

When Adolf Hitler's troops liberated the German Sudetenland in 1938 and finally conquered all of Czechoslovakia, he also came to claim and conquer me, an unwanted and rebellious young teenage orphan girl. After giving me one year of concentrated training and brainwashing in a Nazi youth-leadership school in Prague, Adolf Hitler got from me what my foster-father never managed to get: unquestioning obedience and total willingness to follow his orders. Adolf Hitler's words became truth and law to me; he was my god and I trusted him.

Why? *Because he wanted me.* Nobody else had ever needed or wanted me before. Adolf Hitler believed in me! Nobody but my foster-mother had done that before, and my mother was always outvoted by her family when she tried to stick up for me.

"You are my Hitler Youth," Adolf Hitler would say to us in his many speeches. "I believe in you and I claim you, for you are the Germany of tomorrow, you are *my* Germany of tomorrow. In you, the young people, the Thousand-Year Reich has its roots and hopes!"

With millions of others in the ranks of our Hitler Youth, I laid my will, my heart, my emotions, and my life at Hitler's feet. In all sincerity I believed I was doing the right thing. How glad I was that I had finally learned what was most important in my life: willing obedience and total commitment to an immortal cause.

How, then, could my eighteen-year-old mind now, all at once, grasp what had happened—the cruel fact that everything I thought to be right was suddenly wrong, that black was white, while white didn't even exist anymore? More mature minds than mine could not handle the unexpected blow that Hitler and the eternal Reich had died. These disillusioned ones decided to die also, following Adolf Hitler's example and his last orders: *"Wir müssen entweder siegen oder untergehen* [We must either be victorious or go down forever]." I wondered if I should do the same.

During the weeks that followed the collapse of Nazi Germany, reports multiplied that whole families had committed suicide either by poison or gun. It sounded good to me. The bitter disappointment, the pain of hunger, and the terror of Russian occupation were enough to make me long for an end to my life.

There was only one problem. I had made no provision for either poison or gun, as had some Nazi leaders, because I had never questioned Germany's victory! When the breakdown came, it was too late to secure these means of an "honorable death"—and it was unthinkable for me that I could die any other way but *den Ehrentod* (the death of honor). Adolf Hitler and his mistress, Eva Braun, had died that way. Rumors had it that Eva took a fast-acting poison. Hitler shot himself. I never doubted those stories for they were in harmony with the Nazi ethics I still lived by. A true, proud Nazi German could not die *den Strohtod* (the straw death) of shame where he (or she) would just lie on his bed of straw waiting for death or his enemies to claim him. Neither could he hang himself like a common jailbird, or choose any form of suicide which was not absolutely foolproof. A German Nazi had to die fearlessly: erect, master of his fate, by his own decision to the last moment—going under with pride and contempt toward death and toward his hated enemies.

Because I could not die the honor death of a Nazi, I *lived*. At least my body did. My mind and emotions turned numb and felt more and more dead. I had lost my ability to reason things out and I felt like two persons. One watched the other in utter disbelief, wondering why I had become a robot in a nightmare of horror. That sensation deepened when, a few weeks after the end of World War II, I found myself in a Communist labor camp in Bohemia. As a Nazi, I had believed in the innate nobleness of human beings—at least as far as the Germanic, Aryan races were concerned. Now, for the first time in my life, I had to see with my own eyes that men could be inhuman. As I watched Russians rape my best girl friend, as I looked into the cold eyes of our cruel overseer who refused water even for a fainting girl, something happened to me. Two emotions came alive within me. The first was my Nazi pride, a pride that went hand in hand with contempt and hate toward the enemies of Nazi Germany.

Up to the end of the war I had acknowledged hate and pride in a theoretical sense as numbers two and three on the Nazi scale of virtues. Number one went to the highest virtue of self-sacrifice as the most noble fulfillment for a human being. Self-sacrifice was no longer needed. What was there left to self-sacrifice for? Hate and pride I knew only on an idealistic level. It wasn't until I watched human beings be *in*human that something snapped in me. Hate and pride then became fact—became a real part of me.

Let it never be said that raw hate cannot keep a person going! Hate gave me strength, fire, and a new fearlessness to outsmart my persecutors. Hate and pride motivated me to walk out of that camp and take a large group of other German women with me when I finally escaped. Hate kept me going when I decided to leave my homeland and flee into Western Germany. Hate can propel a starving body through weeks of rain and through all of Eastern Germany. But what a price one has to pay for such fierce hatred. Hate burns ideals and positive thinking to ashes—and it happens *fast*.

Six months after the end of World War II I found myself, for the first time, free and in Western Germany. The struggle was over. Or was it? To be sure, I wasn't hunted anymore. I was allowed to wander as I pleased. My hate had burned itself out (or so it seemed). The attitude of the West Germans toward us was almost human. Indifferent, perhaps, but nearly human. So why hate?

Then came a day when I took a look into my innermost self, and the changes I saw frightened me. All my idealism was gone, replaced by a deep disillusionment. I distrusted humanity as a whole, and individually. Too numb to feel either sorrow or joy, I did feel a deep resentment toward *any* human philosophy, toward any great cause. I was still terribly confused, but one guiding principle had already begun to emerge in my mind for the rebuilding of my shattered life. It was this: I would never, never again trust myself to anything or any human philosophy. I would content myself with trying to make a decent, honest living—but no more! The price was too high for me to ever live for and dedicate myself to anything greater than just plain, normal living and a family of my own.

I did not change that basic attitude after I married and even after I finally found my way back to the church of my childhood. It all seemed to fall into a very sensible pattern. Was it not only decent for me to serve God, when I finally realized that it was He who had watched over my battered life? As a child I had lived by my mother's God-concept. As a teenager I gave myself to Adolf Hitler. Life was a learning pattern and I had changed gods several times. It might sound terrible, but it was ever so true. I had changed from the God of my childhood to the German god, Adolf Hitler—and now back to that Christian God and true Sovereign Ruler of the Universe. It felt right to serve God in the secure setting of a church and to earn my way to heaven. It seemed very prudent, rather logical, comfortable; and I had finally found my desired, quiet, and secure way of life.

I buried my memories in my subconscious and refused to ever think about the bad ones. My hate and pride had burned themselves out, or so I thought. My family and I lived a decent life. We did unto others as they did unto us. My husband and I held church offices; we also paid our dues to God and the government. Little by little we worked ourselves up to a respectable, middle-class social level in postwar Germany and felt humbly proud of it. We had hoped to do so in America someday, but nothing had ever come of that dream and our future seemed rather predictable, uneventful, and laid out. The time had come when I could forget my nightmares, nurse my ulcers back to health, and watch the blue sky of contentment deepen my peaceful, straight path to heaven.

Out of that deep blue sky, in the manner of Saul of Tarsus, I got hit one day by a bolt of spiritual lightning. In the middle of my sunlit path of daily complacency stood *Jesus Christ*. Had He not come my way before? Yes. And every time I saw Him I had managed to walk around Him. (Jesus does not force Himself upon us.)

Why had I evaded Him?

Because I couldn't face Him.

Sure, I talked about Him and confessed Him before the people. I knew well His life story and sayings since my earliest childhood. But He had never been anything more than an historic figure to me. A wonderful Man who had walked the dusty roads of Galilee 2,000 years ago—I couldn't help but admire Him—but that was all!

I never trusted Him or myself enough to make Him my personal Saviour. I understood too well what it would mean. I would have to become like Him. I would have to live and think like Him, and that I simply couldn't do. I couldn't, even if I wanted to!

Two things stood between Him and me—my hate and my pride. But hadn't I left both emotions behind? Were they not burned out? As I had to find out to my dismay, both hate and pride were still very much alive. I kept them well hidden, but they were still around. How they festered in my soul. For I had not changed; I had exchanged. My sinful heart had traded Nazi pride for the subtle pride of humility. I was now truly proud of my great show of Christian humility! As for my hate—it wore now the cloak of righteous anger toward the enemies of God, even toward those who crucified Him. I had changed, but I had never been born again.

"How could You do it, Jesus Christ," I argued as I looked into His face that day when He stood again in my path and I couldn't ignore Him any longer. "How could You *do* it? How can a person love his enemies, You Man on the cross? I cannot do it and I am not so sure I want to! The best I can do is to try to push my painful memories aside and ignore them, but every time I remember the past, my hands form a fist. How can I possibly ever *love* that human beast who raped my best girl friend? How can I have kind thoughts toward that brute of an overseer who delighted in torturing us in that Communist labor camp?

"And as for those who crucified You, Christ—I hate them, too. I even feel resentful that You *let* Yourself be so terribly humiliated. If You had to die for my sins, Son of God, couldn't You have died more proudly? Didn't You have legions of angels at Your command? Why didn't You just wipe out Your persecutors and then You could have died triumphantly, if it was needed."

Jesus Christ must have smiled, I fancy, while He listened patiently to my hot and foolish arguments that day and many days afterwards. He smiled. He understood. And He waited.

Yes, He smiled and waited, for He knew something I didn't know at that time. Christ knew all about hate and pride. He Himself had suffered under it so much while on earth—perhaps He was even tempted by these emotions. He had never yielded—He knew about the force and doggedness of such feelings, but He also knew that something else was stronger: His love!

His love worked on me until my defenses wore thin. I gave in to His wooing, one sleepless night. Under the stars I made peace with Him and gave Him all I had to give. It was not much, and it was a mess! My body was broken and wracked by ulcer pains, my nerves threadbare, my emotions bitter and crippled, my mind confused and full of hang-ups. But I just laid everything—even my hate and pride —in His nail-scarred hands and let Him take over.

I wish I could say that I was changed in an instant that night. But I wasn't! I do not doubt that some people do have this experience, for Christ's love and miracle-power is unlimited. I know that today. But, as we've said, His love never forces, and I was too stubborn to let go all at once. Ever so slowly, Jesus chiseled my pride away; little by little He laid bare the roots of my hate so that I could pull them out. As we walked and talked together from day to day I learned to turn around. It had to be a full 180-degree turn: Christ had to undo my whole Nazi mold. It was hard learning and I often became discouraged—I still do at times—but how exciting it is to learn with Christ!

When Jesus becomes a reality in our lives, we learn to think His thoughts, feel and give His love, and His impulses become ours. The world looks different, for we look at it through new eyes—*His* eyes. We are new creatures in Him, as the Bible tells us (*see* 2 Corinthians 5:17). *Newness.* That's what I needed. No patch-up job, no remodeling of my character and attitudes would have sufficed. I had to be born again: every whit new!

It was certainly in God's wisdom that our remote plans to come to America didn't materialize until I had found this new life in Christ. I know today that I could never have survived in the New World without knowing Him. When I left Germany with my family in 1955 to come to America, I thought I had learned most of what there is to learn about being a new woman in Christ. Little did I know what lay ahead of me.

To most immigrants, America is immediately overwhelming. I've discussed this with numerous immigrants who confirmed my own feelings on the subject. It's almost like stepping on the shores of an entirely different world. Perhaps the astronauts had this sensation when they stepped onto the moon. Certainly America was another planet to me when we arrived. It was all the more so, perhaps, because of my peculiar background. How do you think America looks to a girl who spent her childhood in a hayloft, her teen years in a Nazi school and a Communist labor camp, and her young-adult years as a refugee in postwar Germany? How does America look to one who had never known affluence—freedom—democracy and—garbage cans.

That is what this book is all about.

1

Someday . . .

Propellers hummed our plane westward through the night, while the new morning dawn tried to catch up with us.

My husband and our two children slept in their seats but I was wide-awake. I looked down the dimly lit aisle and watched all those sleeping faces of my fellow emigrants. How could they all sleep when we were only hours away from entering the United States of America? I felt much too excited and full of anticipation to even close one eye.

Maybe none of these others had dreamed and longed as I had, for so many years, to come to America. Ever since that unforgettable morning when, by sheer accident, I had met those first American soldiers, I had felt that strange tug to see America. That was long ago and those events seemed almost unreal in my memory. Not that I could ever forget them, but it all appeared so far away right now—and stranger than fiction.

Had I really ever been that homeless, hunted refugee girl who had fled out of Czechoslovakia toward the West after World War II was over? Yes, I was that refugee or I wouldn't be sitting on this plane right now. Each one of us aboard was a refugee from Eastern Europe. That was one of the things that made us eligible for this emigrant flight. How long I had waited and prayed for this to happen! For long years it looked as though it would never come to pass. My husband's and my own war records had been too much against us.

At the end of World War II, Rudy had been a second commander on a big Nazi U-boat and I a rather high-ranked Nazi youth leader. After the collapse of Nazi Germany we both had suffered at the hands of the victorious armies. Rudy was lucky. He managed to get out of his English prisoner-of-war camp within a few weeks and get to Western Germany without much trouble. I was too far East to get away from the Russians and I was caught by them. Was I ever! Caught in the turmoil of Russian occupation, caught to do slave labor for the Communists in Bohemia, caught in my own confusion, and the horrible disappointment of the collapse of my beloved Reich.

Would I ever be able to forget my horrid flight from the East to the West Zone? Rain, endless rain and no raincoat; hunger, gnawing hunger and no food but herbs and a few roots and mushrooms, for long weeks. Cold, wet, pitch-dark nights and no shelter. Nobody bothered to open a home to us, or a barn, a hayloft, or anything else!

Three million refugees (as later statistics brought out)—three million women, children, and old people walked through Eastern Germany that summer of 1945 trying to get to the West. No men, of course, for any man who had been strong enough to carry a gun had been ordered to the fighting fronts, up to the last days of the war. They had not yet returned when the trek to the West was on. German men were either dead or in prisoner-of-war camps that first postwar summer, and a convulsing, defeated nation lay paralyzed while we refugees walked.

I think I know the sensation a doe must feel when she is chased by hunters and finally sees herself surrounded. I was that dumb, frightened, living thing one long night ago when I found myself caught in a death trap at the end of Communist no-man's-land. I wasn't alone. Many refugees had tried with me to break through to Western Germany that dark, foggy night, but fate seemed against us. Morning dawn moved faster than we did and the Russian patrol discovered us before we had made it across to the other side. I believe I know, also, how a hedged-in animal feels as he makes one last desperate attempt to break out and get away. I did just that. There was nothing to lose and I knew it. I was not only responsible for myself, but for my girl friend and a strange child I had picked up in the dark woods while trying to get away myself. The three of us fought time, distance, flood waters, and a steep hill while we were exhausted—and made it to the West!

And what was on the Western side? That long-ago, weary morning I had no idea! Rumors behind the Iron Curtain had it that the American military zone of Western Germany was a good place for refugees. That's why I had tried for it, but I was far from being convinced that the good reports had to be true! After all, weren't the Americans allies of the Russians? They'd hated us enough to come across the big ocean to fight us. They were the ones who had tipped the scale toward Germany's defeat. How I hated them! I hated all those vultures who had clawed Germany to pieces. I detested them! I feared them! I was as much afraid of the Americans as I was of the Russians.

I will *never* forget the horror I felt when, one hour after we had crossed the border, I knocked on a door and an American soldier opened it. I would have never knocked on anybody's door if it had not been for that strange little child. She was so cold and drenched and pale—I feared for her life.

The American soldiers took us into their barracks that morning. They gave us food, shelter, warmth, and *smiles*. I watched their every move with deep suspicion. All I wanted was to get away from them before they could hurt us.

No Russian or any other soldier had touched me so far and I was determined to keep it that way. I knew I would rather die than let myself be raped. I was hysterical with fear and ready to fight, claw, scream, and bite. . . .

The propellers hummed and I smiled to myself. Who would have thought that ten years later I'd find myself in a plane as an emigrant to the United States of America! Thank you, friendly American soldiers! But for you I would never have wanted to come to America. What if you had attempted what I feared? But you didn't!

I shall never forget what I saw when we three girls finally walked away from that GI barracks. Our clothing was dry, our stomachs full, and my muscles tight. I was still defensive and ready to fight. When I finally dared to stop and look back, I couldn't believe my eyes.

Nobody had come after us to grab us: nobody! There was that drab, long building nestled among evergreen trees in the heart of Germany, and out of every window and door we saw waving arms and smiling young faces. Laughter, shouts, and words we didn't understand floated toward us, and I heard myself say, *"Danke, danke schön, danke* [Thank you].*"*

I wanted to say more, but I couldn't. I spoke German, Czech, and a bit of Russian, but no English! Even if I had spoken English, I might not have known what to say: not then! We walked away from those first Americans I had ever met and I was at war with myself. A conflict raged within me and I felt my head swim. . . . Those American soldiers puzzled me. Who were they?

> **What made them so jolly and human?**
> **Were all Americans like these young men?**
> **How could I hate them?**
> **Had the Nazis lied about America and Americans to me?**
> **Did Americans have something I didn't know about? What was it?**

I walked away that day and those young GI's could not know what they had done for me, a poor refugee. They had given me more than food and shelter—they had kindled a spark of hope in my nearly dead heart. I knew then—ten long years ago—that *someday* I would go to America and find answers to my many questions. One day I would find out what made Americans different. Whatever it was, *I liked it!*

Someday I *had* to go and see America. Someday—sometime.

2

They Call It Garbage

The time had come. The giant plane landed and a multitude of dazed immigrants disembarked. Pushing and shoving with their luggage, they boarded busses waiting to take them to the railroad station. My children snuggled close to me; everything looked so strange and different. I smiled reassuringly and pointed toward the white box that each of us carried. The stewardess had handed one to every passenger as we left the plane.

"Open it," I said in German. "Let's see what it is!"

We each opened our box and my children crooned with delight. What a beautiful sight! On white paper napkins were two sandwiches separately wrapped in transparent paper, a red apple in a soft wrapping of special design, a brown-sugar-frosted cupcake with a white paper collar, and several candies individually wrapped in colorful, shiny wrappers. It all looked so perfect and beautiful that I had a hard time unwrapping and eating it. I wondered if I should hold on to it as a keepsake of our arrival in America. Well, we were hungry enough to eat it all. Then I encountered my first perplexity in America! What was there to do with four white empty boxes, eight sandwich wrappers (which we folded carefully for reuse), and all the other leftover papers and unused napkins we suddenly found on our hands?

It honestly never entered my head that we could throw it away! Why would anyone in his right mind throw away anything that could be reused? Little did I know then about the germ-consciousness of an affluent American nation. I looked, puzzled, at the shower of paper and cardboard in our laps and thought of the two tightly filled suitcases, our only possession, but too full to hold the extra gift of varied papers from the airline!

25

The charter bus stopped and the immigrants filed out, one by one, passing a large container provided by the airline. The bus personnel motioned to us to drop our white boxes into that container. Obediently we did so. *Of course,* I thought, *the airline wants those things back so they can use them for the next load of people. How dumb of me to think that we should hold on to them forever!*

It didn't dawn on me till later that the containers we dropped our boxes into were garbage cans. Nor did I know then that the airline would have been in serious trouble if they had reused these things, for America has strict sanitary-food laws—and big garbage cans!

Dear me! I had never seen a big garbage can before in my life. Little refuse baskets in the German cities are big enough to hold only cigarette butts and ashes. Up to that moment I didn't know that paper could be just thrown away. Paper, to me, had to be folded, put away, reused, and at last given up to kindle a fire. Food leftovers were eaten, and potato peelings, eggshells, and such stuff buried in the ground to improve the soil for growing food—I didn't know there was such a thing as garbage.

I soon found out. I also quickly discovered that Americans don't always bother to throw the stuff called garbage into those monstrous cans of theirs. We arrived at the railroad terminal and I was aghast! Was *this* America? The place was dirty, strewn with litter, dumped newspapers, and other such things. Why did the people leave their newspapers on the seat and just go away? Didn't they want to take it home and use it? Were they not at least proud enough to keep a public place picked up?

Overtired and afraid, my children huddled still closer to me. There was so much noise that I wondered: *Do Americans love noise?* They seemed to love not only noise, but color, electric lights, and advertisements. Wherever I looked, something seemed to either scream or flash at me—but it didn't make any sense.

What a feeling of isolation and loneliness one can have when letters of the alphabet have no meaning and words are like the sound of running water! We had to wait several hours for our train to Michigan, and my husband had left to explore New York. Weariness crept over my tired body and the first pangs of homesickness needled me.

What in the whole wide world had possessed us to leave our cozy little house, a good job, and our loved ones to come to such a strange, foreign country? I knew already that I could *never* feel at home here, *never* learn that horrible language, and *never* accept some of the things I saw.

The sinking sensation in my stomach deepened when my little boy had to go "somewhere." *Oh,* I sighed, *where did I have my head?* Why didn't it dawn on me while we were still in Germany that I had no business going to another land where I couldn't even find a public toilet?

An elderly gentleman who spoke both German and English, sensing my plight, pointed to a door marked WOMEN, and after some anxious moments my son and I felt much better. We turned to wash our hands and what a pleasant surprise was ours! The place provided not only running water, but liquid soap, and paper towels—free!

While I scrubbed my boy and myself, I tried to figure it all out. Who paid for all of that? Why would anybody do such a thing? It must cost lots of money to keep such a place supplied. How come people didn't appreciate it? Paper towels were strewn everywhere and the place was littered.

Yes, America must be rich or Americans wouldn't throw so much stuff around. Strangely enough, that thought gave me a lift. With a new bounce in my step I walked back to the luggage. America had many new things—among them a thing called garbage—it was everywhere.

3

Never-Ever Time

American garbage. Something that belongs either in big cans or gets stored in garages. *Garbage. Garage.* The words sound the same; they belong together. Except sometimes garbage is also called *junk.*

People remember by association, and I surely did, as I learned English. It was one thing to hear and remember a word and another thing to make it meaningful to my own understanding. I know today that I was puzzled by things to which Americans have never given a second thought. I will never forget that train trip to Michigan from New York. The country flew by and though I hadn't slept for twenty-four hours I was too afraid to miss anything, so I didn't take a nap. I kept my eyes glued to the window. The countryside was pretty, even similar to my homeland, but how come there were so many old shacks among the trees? Surely, in America where people are rich, nobody would live in such old weather-beaten huts—or would they? We saw lots of fancy houses and farms, too—but these I expected to see.

One thing puzzled me even more than the extreme housing styles of America: the contraption on top of nearly every building—a very high and elaborate lightning rod! Not only did it have one metal point to divert dangerous lightning, but it had metal arms sticking out on both sides. Were there that many thunder-and-lightning storms in America that every home needed such a fancy device? Would we have to have such a thing on our place, too? Would the authorities perhaps force us to get it right away? If they did, I hoped it wasn't too expensive. We had only one hundred dollars to start out with.

I voiced my thoughts to my husband. He shook his head and said, "I don't think that those are all lightning rods. I think it has something to do with *Fernsehen* [television]."

I mused, "Rudy, that doesn't make any sense. If those old shacks are homes and people live in them, they must be poor people. How could they be so rich as to own a television? If they cannot afford to fix or paint their houses, how can they afford such luxuries?"

My husband didn't know, and we just wondered.

We wondered about more things when we finally arrived at our sponsor's place. (A primary requirement for immigrating to America is a sponsor—this is to guarantee that the immigrants will not become public charges.) Ours were an elderly couple, the husband in the construction business. They had a fine home at the outskirts of town and they came with a big car to pick us up. The man opened the large car trunk to stash our luggage. Rudy handed him our two suitcases. One contained clothing for the four of us, the other was filled with books.

"Is that *all?*" the sponsor asked my husband.

"Yes," Rudy said, "that's all."

We arrived at the house and the table was set for us for a very late breakfast. I remember two things from that first breakfast menu which puzzled me. The first was that each of us had half a grapefruit beside the cereal bowl. We had never tasted grapefruit before, and little Michael squinted because it tasted so sour. The sponsor watched us.

"Put sugar on it," he motioned, "or you can sprinkle salt on it to cut the sourness—whichever you like best!"

Rudy translated. Salt on fruit? Yes, I learned fast that Americans put salt on and into almost anything—watermelon, meats, a meticulously prepared meal—they do not savor the various flavors of different foods—it is salt, pepper, and sugar en masse with everything! The other puzzle was the bread. I had wondered about it once before. Those first American soldiers we had run into years ago had given us breakfast, too. Among all the strange things we three girls ate that long-ago morning was some white, soft baked goods which looked like *Kuchen* (cake) but it wasn't sweet. Now we had the same thing offered to us again.

I looked at our sponsor. He had a German background and understood some of my German words. *"Brot?"* I asked hesitatingly. The man nodded. Yes, it was bread, at least to him. He showed me the wrapper: WONDER BREAD.

I nodded. Yes, I understood. For once, no puzzle there! Wonder is *Wunder* in German and I understood why Americans called their bread a wonder—it was a total wonder to me that they could exist on such spongy, gooey stuff. I was greatly disturbed to think that I would never again have a crust of real *Brot*—dark, strong in taste, with a hard crust and a hearty bite to it. The thought only added to the deep homesickness which had hit me again as we sat at the unfamiliar table.

"Mary," the lady of the house said and Rudy translated, "I hope the closet in your bedroom is big enough for the four of you. I have so much stuff in the other bedrooms that I couldn't make any more room for you."

"Thank you, it is more than enough," Rudy assured her and told me what was said.

I looked around in that big house as we were shown to our bedrooms, and said softly, "Rudy, why do two people need so much stuff?"

Our sponsor overheard me though I spoke in German and he answered for Rudy, who translated. "Tell your wife that it is a good question, but it's hopeless! My wife is a pack rat and the only solution to our problem is a good fire. Wait until you see the garage—we have so much junk stored there that we have to park our cars in the driveway!"

I saw the garage and I was overwhelmed. I never questioned that it was wise to save everything, but why so much of it and for what purpose? And why did my sponsor call the stuff in the garage *junk* and the junk in the extra closets *stuff?*

And why do Americans have too many hangers in every closet? I had never seen metal hangers before; neither had I seen built-in closets. I unpacked our two suitcases. Our few belongings didn't fill even half of the closet and looked rather forlorn. I couldn't find bookshelves so I put our books into the chest of drawers. I had hardly any other things to put into it, anyway. The sponsor showed his smiling face again. "Would your children like to take a bath?" he asked.

I smiled back. Would they! Their weekly bath was one of their favorite pastimes, and we all felt sticky from our long trip.

The bathroom lifted my spirits again. What a luxury! Hot water out of the faucet. I thought of how hard I had worked in Germany to heat up enough bathwater in the washhouse for all four of us, and even that had been so much easier than what I had as a little girl. Mother had to heat the water on the wood stove. Now I watched hot water run out of the faucet. Of course, I wouldn't use too much. I didn't want to get our sponsors upset by taking advantage of their hospitality. I ran a few inches of water into the tub and undressed both children. They climbed in together and squealed with delight. The lady of the house stuck her head through the half-open door and seemed to hide a frown.

Oh dear, I thought, *she is upset with me. What did I do wrong? Did I use too much water?*

Often, in the days to come, I wondered why she frowned so much. When I washed dishes for her she got really perturbed. The more she frowned, the harder I tried to be more saving with hot water and soap—until she finally said what was bothering her: I wasn't using *enough* hot water to suit her concepts of hygiene. Also, I shouldn't undress the children in front of each other . . . and also . . . and also. . . .

Misunderstandings deepened, and today I understand why. How could she know that I bathed my boy and girl in the same bathwater because I tried to be considerate of her hot-water bill? How could she sense *my* perplexity when she herself poured soap into the dishwater until I wondered how I would ever get all that soap off those dishes? I could taste the soap on my plate and on the silverware as we would use it again. I disliked the soap taste mixed in with the food. *No wonder Americans killed the taste of it with large amounts of salt.* But I liked too-much salt even less than I liked soap.

It was a dreadful summer. I just couldn't get used to sticky heat, mosquitoes, popcorn—and a hundred other new things. "Oh, Lord," I would cry over and over again, *"please* let me go home. I'll never fit into this land; it's all so strange to me. I shall never complain again if I can only go home—even if we live on bread and salt—as long as it is dark, hard, real bread!"

Oh, dear, how ungrateful and demanding can immigrants be! Don't they appreciate and realize how good they have it in America?

No, *I* didn't! I was too homesick to be rational and all I knew was that I would never, never like America—***ever.***

4

The Dumb Year

Immigrants call the first year in America "the dumb year." I had more than a dumb year; mine was perplexed and a search in the dark. I was sure that we had misunderstood God's direction and that we had made a great mistake. I wondered if we would have to suffer for it for the rest of our lives—perhaps even die soon—or if God would give us another chance and permit us to go back home. It seemed like God had forsaken us. But why? Because we disobeyed Him? If so, we hadn't done it deliberately! We *thought* it His will when we came to America.

I couldn't feel the presence of God anymore and I panicked. Were we lost? I cried and I prayed and there seemed to be no answer. I kept on praying, crying, wondering—nothing made sense to me anymore—but I tried to live one day at a time. It wasn't easy! I cried about every little problem.

I cried when the sponsor lady showed me how to do the family wash. She filled warm water into a machine and added soap and then dumped the dry clothing right into it. I shook my head defensively as I watched. Anybody in his right mind knew that wash had to be soaked in *cool water with soda* for at least a night, before it could be washed. This way, she was burning the dirt right into the fibers! My English was too poor to explain such a complicated process, and I tried to gesture my convictions. We had no communication. More frowns and more tears!

"Oh, she is ruining the few things we own. What do I do when our clothing gives out?"

Strangely enough, the laundry looked rather clean when it came from the line, but notwithstanding, I swore I would never wash the American way.

I also swore I would never use a can opener. What a lazy way to cook! Didn't those American housewives have any pride? After I had recovered from the shock of seeing my first supermarket, I formed my own ideas about American food. They had too much of it and most of it was in cans and plastic. I would never use canned goods; I would never become a lazy housewife. One of the first jokes I heard in America was told to me by another immigrant. An American mother called her little son for dinner. The boy shook his head. "How can dinner be ready?" he asked. "I have your can opener!"

I thought that joke so funny, I laughed about it for days. There wasn't much else to laugh about! I would try to tell it to some Americans, but I got mostly blank looks in return. My English was obviously too poor to make a point—or couldn't they laugh about a good joke when they heard it?

The first three words that made a lasting impression in my befuddled mind were *dollar, sale,* and *diet.* These words are used more in American conversation, I found, than any other, and I soon learned to pick them out of the stock of words which passed my ears without meaning. It wasn't too long before I knew that *dollar* wasn't just money. Dollar was a way of life, an attitude, a value qualification, and the measure of most things. Food *sales* made people fat, and other sales filled the garages with junk and the closets with stuff. The sale things were generally of no use to the buyer, but, I observed, Americans buy them in the hope that someone else might someday be able to use them, mainly at Christmas. Then they wrap an item which cost only pennies in a box and gift wrap which cost dollars, and give it to somebody they like.

Another word for sale is *bargain.* That word has almost as much magic as the word *dollar.* Americans love bargains. I will never forget the time when our sponsor lady came home with a bulky chair for the living room. I stared in unbelief. Where would she put that chair—the place was so overstuffed with furniture already?

She shuffled everything around until she found a place to squeeze it in. All smiles, she looked triumphantly into my face: "I couldn't let it go, Mary," she said elated. "It was such a bargain. I paid only ten dollars."

I nodded and fought tears again. Was I coveting her chair because we had absolutely nothing? Maybe she thought so, but truly I didn't! I cried at the thought of where those ten dollars came from. My husband had worked for only a short time as a carpenter's helper for our sponsor, when he cut his hand. We had neither workmen's compensation nor medical insurance, and there was no income. I went to work so we could pay rent to our sponsor—ten dollars a week for the bedroom we lived in.

The only jobs I found were strawberry picking and housecleaning. It took me several days to earn ten dollars. "*Only* ten dollars" to buy a bargain. I couldn't see it this woman's way; my back hurt too much. On the other hand, my sponsor lady couldn't understand my delight when I came home one evening from a housecleaning job and dragged in some boxes. She raised her eyebrows. I bubbled with joy. In my broken English I tried to tell her that the lady had given me several boxes of clothing instead of money for my work. What a bargain!

Both our sponsor and his wife shook their heads. "No, no, Mary," the wife said with a big frown, "don't you let them do that to you. They are taking advantage of you!" My husband translated. I looked, surprised, from one face to the next. Didn't they understand? My boss *gave* me all that clothing.

"Is it stuff that will fit you?" my husband asked.

"Oh, no," I shook my head," it is not for me!" I wanted to send it to Germany for the Hungarian refugees who were just then flooding Austria and southern Germany after the revolution.

The faces softened. "We will give you more clothing when you are ready to send it," the couple said, "but don't take old clothing in place of pay. They are just trying to get rid of their junk!" (That word *junk* again!)

The word must have spread throughout the neighborhood that I was planning to send warm clothing to refugees in Germany. More and more people brought clothing to us, week after week, even after we had moved out of our sponsors' bedroom into a basement apartment in the slums. From there, God and some kind Christians rescued us into a new beginning. We moved twice and found another basement to live in. But wherever I moved, my many boxes of clothing moved right along with me. By November of that year, nearly six months after we had arrived in America, we had so much clothing in our basement that we had to climb over boxes to go to bed. The time had come to ship it. Winter was coming and the refugees needed those things. How helpful all those Americans were! They had brought so many fine things, even two old fur coats. The only thing they had forgotten in all their happy giving was—Who would pay the postage? It would have never dawned on me to mention it to anybody; after all, they had been so kind and given us so much already.

It took me several days to sort and pack all those donations. I had to move slowly because I was pregnant and constantly sick. But I finally had it all wrapped up for overseas shipping. Twelve large boxes waited to go to the post office of the little Michigan town we lived in.

My husband took off an hour early from his construction work to make it to the post office before closing time. It was payday and he had cashed his check so that we could use part of the money to pay the shipping.

I felt a bit apprehensive. I had no idea what the postage for that large shipment would be, but I was sure it would take the bigger part of the paycheck. The postmaster weighed and checked it, and we filled out all the forms he handed to us. Then he quoted the price. Our faces fell. The postage was not only *part* of our weekly paycheck: it was *all* we possessed *and six dollars more.* My husband and I looked at each other. He knew what I was thinking and he nodded. Turning to the postmaster he pulled out his pay envelope and said, "Sir, these packages go to Germany to help Hungarian refugees through the winter. We are new in America and have no savings. This money here is my paycheck and we have no more than this. We are six dollars short. We give you all we have. Would you either hold one package or ship it all now and allow us to bring you the remaining six dollars next week, please?"

I held my breath and watched that postmaster's sober face. Would he cooperate? It was *so* important to send it all—and now. The refugees needed it.

The man gave us a long, strange look. Then he reached into his pocket for his billfold, took six dollars out and said quietly: "I will pay the extra six dollars for you. The packages will all be shipped today; don't worry at all. Never mind the six dollars, either. You don't need to bring it next week—it's all paid."

We thanked that kind man over and over, then we turned to go back to our basement. I smiled at Rudy. "Don't worry about food for next week, dear. I still have a few things in the cupboard. We will make it," I assured him. "We have lived on small fare before!"

Nobody knew about our food problem. We didn't tell anybody about the postage. Didn't the Bible say that when you do a kindness, to do it secretly and not even tell your left hand what your right hand is doing? Well, I wasn't so confident in my heart as I acted before my family. Our food supply was dwindling faster than I thought, and by the middle of the week I wondered how I could possibly stretch it much farther. That night, as we sat around our evening meal of soup and potatoes, we heard a loud knock at the door. I went to answer it but nobody was there. I looked into the darkness and listened. What was going on? I stepped out to look some more and almost fell over it! Beside the door stood a big box filled to the brim with lots of things. It was so heavy I couldn't lift it. My husband came and helped to carry it in. What was it? *Food!* Lots and lots of food: cans and more cans, and an envelope with five dollars in it.

Who had done such a kind thing for us? Who knew that we were almost out of food? Nobody knew it but God. That was enough, more than enough! We had so much food that week and the following weeks that I felt guilty when I thought of the Hungarian refugees. We didn't know then what a Thanksgiving holiday was, but the Americans did. And we were learning that Americans do not only prepare Thanksgiving dinner for themselves; they also prepare Thanksgiving baskets for the needy. Someone felt impressed to leave such a love gift at our doorstep and walk away before we could tell him our thanks.

God must have smiled. He did not only provide abundantly; He also taught me a very big lesson.

The next day I walked to the store to buy a can opener!

What is it that the old American proverb says: "Be careful what you say or you may have to eat your words."

How many *nevers* would I have to eat?

As many as there were cans in that box—and more.

Whenever I meet new immigrants and they ask me for advice, I tell them with a smile: "Don't ever say *never*. Wait until the "dumb year" is passed before you decide what you like or dislike. America is like the weather—if you don't like it, wait awhile. . . ."

5

The American Dream

Two years of struggle and two more babies later we found ourselves in California. My husband worked for a Christian sales organization and through them he bought our first house. At last we were on the way to fulfill the American Dream.

What is the American Dream? To be rich and happy, of course. Millions of people dream that dream. All over the globe, people dream of going to America and becoming rich. It's riches that make people happy, everybody knows that. I dreamed for many long years about it and now we watched our dream come true. Proudly I wrote back home. We owned a house and a car! How about that!

Of course I was careful not to tell a few details that our German relatives could have never fully understood. The free-enterprise system and the buy-now-and-pay-later habits of the New World were literally unknown in Europe at that time. It would have been wasted effort to explain in my letters that the mortgage company provided the money and we a signature to make us look rich back home. We were also careful not to mention that we were always only one month and one missed car-or-house payment away from being poor again. Why worry them? We worried enough about that ourselves at the end of every month, and to my surprise I found out that being rich did not make us instantly happy.

It puzzled me and I thought about it while we moved into our new house. It had four bedrooms, two baths, dark brown linoleum floors, no stove, no washing machine, no curtains and no furniture.

Maybe I wasn't happy because I wasn't rich enough yet, I thought. It had never before dawned on me that riches had *degrees.* For me, to be rich meant possessing a house and a garden and a car. Now I had all three. To be sure, the house was empty—the yard was dry, chalky fill dirt with no topsoil, grass, or landscaping—and our black Volkswagen was too small to fit the family into without some sweating and elbow pushing.

I did some praying in order to find the needed solutions: "Jesus," I prayed, "a house is obviously not enough. I need a stove, a table, some chairs, a couch, beds and please—a washing machine."

Yes, a washing machine! That was another "never" I had swallowed long before that time. I learned to appreciate the "lazy" ways of washing endless diapers, towels, sheets, and dirty pants. I was busy enough just pinning them on the line for drying.

The Lord smiled as He had before, and gave me what I asked for. God bless the American people for their willingness to share! Within a few months our house was filled with furniture, our closets with *stuff* and the garage with *junk*. The little Volkswagen had to be parked outside. Now I could be happy! But I wasn't! The Lord and I had another talk.

"Lord," I said, "I don't want to sound ungrateful or greedy, but I think I need more carpeting in this house. Those kids track dirt in all day long because there is no grass in our yard yet—we need a lawn, too—and Lord, could I have a better couch in the living room, please? It's embarrassing when people come to visit and I have to ask them to sit only at the left side of our couch because they would fall through to the floor at the right end."

A few days after that prayer, I had a lady visitor. Her husband worked in the same sales organization as Rudy did and she knew what it meant to live without a regular income. Our men were paid only by commission. We lived by faith and had no steady paychecks. We knew better than to go out and buy "on time." (There is a difference between faith and presumption!) The house and car payments worried us enough every month. Though the Lord had never let us down so far, I always dreaded the end of every month.

My friend and I talked and I apologized for all the dirt tracks on the dark brown linoleum floor. Oh, if I just could find some used floor covering somewhere!

"Mary," she said, "I saw something the other day that could be of use to you. Carpet dealers and factories always have carpet samples on hand. These are small squares of various floor coverings which they show to their customers. When they change the stock they discard the old samples. Go around and see if you couldn't buy those cheaply. Then find old rugs that people throw away, buy a good glue, and start creating your own special carpet by pasting those squares on top of any old floor cover."

What fun I had for weeks after her visit which helped carpet my house. My floor looked "different," to say the least. Perhaps it could be best described as a giant chessboard, and I sometimes wonder if my two sons became avid chess players because my carpets conditioned them squarely toward it!

I also planted a lawn and many trees and rosebushes. How glad I was for sales—once in a while they really can be of some use. One day someone brought me an almost-new couch and matching chair —in a deep luscious green. It looked so rich on top of my checkered carpet. Now I had finally arrived and could be happy!

I was not, and I had a reason for it.

"Lord," I said one evening, "I am so grateful for all the new carpets You gave me and my almost-new living-room set, but now I have another problem. I need a vacuum cleaner to keep it all clean. The dirt gets between the edges of the squares, and the couch has all those buttons to catch dust. I am also pregnant again and have a hard time crawling on my knees to get to it all."

Only three days later someone gave me a working vacuum cleaner.

I rejoiced and thanked the Lord—and turned around and asked for one more thing. I prayed for a piano so Chris could begin lessons— and I got it! I prayed for more clothing and I got that, too. I prayed and I got, and I prayed and got more. How much I had gotten was apparent when my husband was promoted to a supervisory position and we were transferred to Northern California. The company sent a moving van and our belongings filled the whole thing. The garage junk could hardly be squeezed in on top of it.

How could two suitcases expand and within just five years fill a whole van? We squeezed all our belongings into my new dream house in Northern California. It had everything I ever wanted and some more. Wall-to-wall carpeting, a dishwasher, a fireplace, washer and dryer, a freezer—yes, it had everything to make me happy—but I wasn't.

What was wrong with me?
What was wrong with my American Dream?

6
Only an Apple

I had never noticed it before, but all of a sudden my green couch and chair looked so very shabby on my wall-to-wall carpet. It didn't bother me one bit that our bedroom furniture was far from elaborate; I was glad for just enough beds. But the living room! What would the neighbors think if they saw my faded green couch and chair? The years and five children had been hard on them.

I went to the Lord and told Him that I urgently needed new furniture for the living room. The Lord smiled and gave me something else I needed more, and *first*. He knew that the time had come when I had to learn the secret of real happiness. So He didn't send me the couch I asked for, not then. He sent me to the hospital instead. My stomach ulcer had gotten so bad that the time had come for major surgery. When I woke up from the anesthetic, I found myself hooked to a machine. Some tubes stuck out of my nose and throat. What a nuisance! The machine pumped my stomach day and night. "Lord," I prayed in my daze, "please get me well fast! You know I have to go back home to my five children. My poor husband can't look after them for too long; he wouldn't know how. Also what will happen to my brand-new house and my wall-to-wall carpet?" God didn't answer, not then!

For a week my condition stayed critical and my angry, inflamed throat began to hurt more than the little bit of stomach they had left within me. Those tubes caused my nose and throat to swell shut.

My husband acted almost impatient at the end of the first week.

"What's the matter with you, girl?" he said. "This is not like you. We all expected you to be up and around by now!"

I didn't say too much; I didn't want him to know how much I hurt and how rotten I felt. That night I tossed in pain and without sleep again. I began to plead and argue with the Lord.

"Why did I get so sick, Jesus?" (I knew the answer before He told me.)

"You worry too much, my child."

"Lord," I said through my tears, "what has happened to me? I never had so much in all my life. You have blessed us so much: You answered my prayers so often and people at home think we are rich. But I am not happy—I always worry. What's wrong with me?"

God showed me that night why I was so miserable. Somewhere I had caught the idea that material things could make a person happy, and for several years I had been trying to catch a rainbow. How anxious and overeager I had become, trying to keep up with my neighbors and other immigrants. Had I forgotten how little a human being needs, to be happy? The Lord took me by the hand that night and let me relive some of my past.

I felt again the rain in my face and the gnawing hunger in my ulcered stomach while fleeing westward. Then I saw myself in a warm kitchen. It was my principal's kitchen in Western Germany. I had made it to the safety of the American Zone and had just been hired as a teacher. The school principal and his wife had taken me in until I could find my own lodging. They invited me to eat supper with them. After the simple meal the principal's wife reached into the cupboard and handed me an apple. An apple! How long had it been since I had eaten an apple? I had forgotten how apples tasted.

"Ma'am," I had said to her, "would you permit me to save this apple for a few days so I could enjoy it a bit longer?"

"You eat it," she said, "I will give you another one when you leave!"

I ate that apple. Oh, how good that luscious, aromatic piece of wonder felt in my stomach. Just like sunshine and soft hay and clover in a crisp autumn breeze. How well I remembered. I felt again the deep pang of disappointment when I recalled the tears I fought.

Tears, because she had forgotten to give me that second apple she had promised to me!

"Lord," I said, heartsick and very contrite that pain-racked night, "will You forgive me? And will You help me to see things Your way? I shall never chase after so many things again, Lord, if You get me out of here—and Lord, please, please, can I have an apple? Nothing else, Lord—only an apple!"

I had a bad night and the surgeon arrived early the next morning with a whole group of medical personnel. My bed was surrounded with grave-looking faces. The doctor rattled off orders to his assistant, to the head nurse, the dietitian. . . . I touched his hand.

"Please, doctor," I interrupted him weakly, "may I have an apple?"

The head nurse shook her head and opened her mouth. The surgeon motioned at her and gave me a long, thoughtful look. Then he smiled. "Yes, I will let you have an apple if you promise me to chew it very, very well."

I smiled under my tubes, and tears stung my eyes. "I promise," I whispered hoarsely. "Yes, I promise you!"

"Give her an apple," the doctor said curtly to the head nurse. Her mouth was still open. She nodded with a frown. Everyone left and after a while someone brought me a big golden apple. It took me several hours to eat it all: I chewed it ever so carefully. It felt so cool to my swollen throat and tasted like sunshine, haylofts, golden autumn leaves. . . .

That afternoon I felt so much better that the doctor ordered the tubes removed. A week later I went home. What a happy day it was! My children ran screaming with joy into my open arms. My husband looked so relieved. As I stepped into the living room several neighbors greeted me with big smiles. They sat on my old green couch and everywhere. The house seemed to overflow with ready-to-heat casseroles, flowers, and warm, human concern.

"How do you feel?" everybody asked.

"Great," I said, "I feel just fine!" Someone shoved a chair under me; my knees felt like jelly. I let myself drop and looked around.

Sunshine filtered through the curtains and drew a golden design on my faded furniture and the people. Love made me feel rich and content.

I nodded, fought tears and said, *"Ja,* I feel really fine. I am so happy I don't know what to say. Thank you so very much, everybody —*and thank You, Lord."*

7
Curses and Blessings

Following that illness and hospitalization I did stop chasing after things. But the things didn't stop chasing after me. American people, so I've found, are so very willing to go through their closets and share.

"I need an excuse to buy new silver," one of my friends said. "Would you like my old set?"

Of course, I did. First of all, I never had owned any silver before in my whole life; second, how could I say no and hurt someone's feelings? I never used that silver. It needed too much polishing, but it looked so good in the drawer. So did many other things I got, including those SALE items somebody couldn't resist at first—and later they were gift wrapped for my benefit. All those things were too nice to be discarded, but not practical enough to be of use—so I stored them. What happens when all the cupboards and drawers and closets get too full? Then the American housewife complains about too-little storage space and she either has more storage room built in or she moves to a bigger house. That's what we did and two moves (from a big to a bigger house) later, I threw up my hands and looked at my problems. Every closet had untold hangers full of clothing, packed in too tightly to remain unwrinkled. Some of the stuff hadn't been worn for months because ours is a funny family. Everybody has two or three favorite outfits and those are worn most of the time— the rest of our closets are filled with just-in-case-I-might-need-it stuff. That *case* arrives seldom or never, but the closet doors bulge anyway. The kitchen cupboards were stacked high—as in a restaurant —except that nothing matched. From the china to the pots and pans, it was all odd in size and form, not old enough to be antique, and not new enough to be modern. It didn't bother me too much because

I specialized by then in paper plates. What bugged me was that I didn't know where to store them after I dragged them home by the five hundred (bought ON SALE of course)! Maybe I should try the garage? Oh, no: forget that! I knew from the beginning that garages are built to store junk, as are basements, but it gets ridiculous when one has to climb over bicycles, camping gear, garden tools, old tires, and outdated encyclopedias to get to the washing machine and dryer. I never thought I could develop a phobia—but I did: I found myself constantly watching the garage door. Whenever it was left open I either yelled at the children or ran to close it. After all, what would the neighbors think if they looked into that mess? Worse yet, what if the fire marshall should ever pass through our peaceful residential street and have one peek into such a potential fire hazard? It's no wonder to me that more and more Americans have automatic devices to open and shut their garage doors—it is practically essential to one's peace of mind!

I knew in my heart that I had to make some changes. My birthday was approaching and I wheedled close to my husband. "Guess what I want for my birthday?" Raised eyebrows! "What?" he asked.

"A cleaned-up garage!" A profound silence—and plastic flowers for my birthday. Oh, dear, where do I put them?

Too-many material things can become a burden, and I wondered why. How can things that are good become burdensome? Can good things in *excess* become a curse? My life seemed to be one continuous effort to keep the big overstuffed house in order, run mountains of wash through the appliances, and nag the kids not to be so wasteful with everything! What bothered me most was their apparently total absence of guilt when they *did* waste material things, even food. My children were just like most American people I knew. That attitude had puzzled me ever since I started to interact with my neighbors. Americans are friendly people; they are neighborly, inviting each other for meals and parties and for little coffee chats. I'll never forget the time I stood in a friend's kitchen watching her prepare a dish while we talked. The recipe called for an egg yolk. She cracked an egg, separated the yellow from the white, put the yellow into the mixing bowl, *and dumped the egg white into the sink!*

My heart seemed to skip a beat and I gave a shocked sound. Maybe I wondered if a lightning bolt would strike us right then and there, but nothing happened. My friend looked up, saw my perplexed face and laughed. "Oh, Mary, don't look so upset because I threw an egg white away. It's either now or a few days later when it is all dried up in the refrigerator. It saves me time to throw it away now!"

I nodded. I had learned to be quiet, not only because my English wasn't good enough to start an argument, but because I felt so completely confused. The American way of living and thinking so often made no sense to me. Maybe I was just dumb! I was too embarrassed to ask my friendly neighbor why she couldn't have put the egg white into her refrigerator and used it for another meal *before* it dried up. Neither could I have been able to explain why I so often had a hard time smiling when we were invited to eat dinner at a friend's house. How could I convey to my hostess what those big, full American garbage cans do to me? How could I make her understand that it frightened me to watch people throw food away, dump old shoes and clothing into the refuse, and think nothing of it? Sure, I understood that present-day Americans knew nothing about starvation—not even through the last two World Wars did the New World starve. I was glad for that. But what about the rest of the world? As I learned to read the newspapers, I found, ever so often, reports about famine, drought, refugees, and great poverty in other lands and I would feel overwhelmed for having so much. How come nobody else seemed to feel as I did? How come Americans didn't seem to feel guilty like me whenever I had to discard anything?

It was not until I heard an American educator speak and use the term *ethic of consumption* as a positive means to America's prosperity that I finally caught the first glimpse of understanding. In the interests of the American free-enterprise system it is a virtue to consume, and the more a person consumes the more valuable he is. The thought made me dizzy. No wonder people felt so *right* about wasting everything and anything: no wonder their priority values were so different from mine. To waste was to increase and to prosper —but even after I understood that new concept I could never feel right about it. However, it changed my prayers. The first few years, I would find myself praying over and over, "Please, Lord, don't punish the American people for throwing so much good food away. Don't let them go hungry for it someday; they are good people but so thoughtless!" After I understood that the last few generations had been taught that waste was a virtue, I prayed, "Lord, help the American people, they don't know any better."

The Lord did exactly that. He sent the energy crisis. America is waking up to the fact that Americans (6 percent of the world population) are using 35 percent (or more) of the world's goods and 6 billion people out there have nothing. Is it a wonder that so many nations hate us? Americans often wonder why there is so much hostility toward our nation—and they resent it. I don't like it either, but at least I can understand the reason for it. Those antagonistic people out there are hungry and cold—we are full and comfortable, in spite of the energy crisis! I always wondered why the newspapers called it a crisis: I couldn't help but see it as a blessing and great lesson from a kind God. Through it He is teaching us Americans to waste less, to appreciate more, and to begin conserving what there is left to conserve.

What overwhelms me is God's loving patience! Not through hunger or war, but by an energy crisis, God nudged Americans ever so gently, to count their blessings. Is it any wonder that I have a new prayer of praise in my heart? I say it over and over: "Thank You, God, for the energy crisis. Thank You, loving Jesus, for being so indulgent with us. Thank You for teaching us in love!"

8

No Time

One of the things I dreamed about before I came to America was that I would have more time to do the things I liked to do. After all, back home I'd spend a whole day every week in the washhouse, walk or bicycle for miles to get my daily shopping done, and spend hour after weary hour mending clothing and darning socks. Such things were obsolete in America: my friends wrote so in their letters —so what was there left to do? I would read, paint, go for walks. . . .

Dreams, just dreams, I found out.

"Rudy," I said shortly after we had arrived in America, "what does the word *busy* mean?" The sound of the word had dug into my jumbled mind like a buzzing bee but I couldn't catch the clear meaning of that profusely used word.

My husband thought for a while and smiled: "There is no German word for *busy*, my dear, and I can't even explain it to you. Keep your eyes and ears open and you will catch its meaning someday."

Yes, I soon caught the meaning, and nothing perplexed me more for years. Whenever I wasn't "too busy" I would think about that word and the concept behind it. *Busy* is more than a concept, I found out. It is a life-style, an attitude, and a syndrome. It's a value qualification and a frustration, a blessing and a curse, a contagious disease!

Busy, I discovered fast, had something to do with time, or better said, with *no time.* I have no idea if Americans *ever* had plenty of time; they certainly had run out of it by the time I arrived.

Now, why would Americans have no time? They have washing machines, cans and can openers, cars, telephones, drip-dries, push buttons, and hundreds of other time saving devices. How, I wondered—before I learned for myself—do American women occupy the hours that are used by peasant women of other lands: time consumed in scrubbing wooden floors on their knees, washing by hand, weeding the garden, cutting wood and building fires, doing the family ironing without electricity—all of which I did before I came to this country?

Of course! Americans are in a hurry doing *other* things. They're busy at a second job so that the income from it can purchase more timesaving gadgets. Also, they're busy talking on the telephone. Then, too, they help in community affairs, plan and go to rummage sales, give showers, and take their children everywhere by car. If they can catch a minute they watch TV, and look out for good sales. They also steal the time to put on makeup and put their hair in rollers before they go to the supermarket. They fight for a few moments to have a coffee break and a visit with the neighbor. They rush, speed, and pass that time-fever bug on to their children and everyone else. They try ever so hard to be ahead of time—and never catch up!

I watched myself from year to year being sucked deeper and deeper into the swift current of the busy American life, and fighting it. How does one fight time? Why was I fighting it? How was it I had less time in America than I had before I emigrated? Why couldn't I just refuse to take part in that daily rat race and take my own time?

As soon as I knew the general meaning of the word *busy,* I began to dislike it. On the other hand, there had to be a blessing in it, because I watched some people suffering under the heaviness of too much time on their hands.

My children would groan: "There is nothing to do!" Old people would complain about boredom and loneliness and empty time. No other concept or matter has perplexed me more and for as long a time as the American preoccupation with time. I saw myself forced into it: I learned to hurry like everyone else, I watched my children accept it as a normal way of life, but I could never feel right about it. It was like the virtue of "planned obsolescence" that puzzled me for so long as I tried to understand the American thinking on waste. I sensed that "no time" was an attitude and that Americans had almost a collective conception about it—but what was the key to understanding it?

It was not until I had been in the United States for more than a decade, had received my degrees in counseling from an American college, and was deeply involved in listening to and educating young people, that I found my answer to those penetrating questions. One afternoon I sat across from a young woman in her mid-twenties. She was beautiful, carefully groomed, well educated, very articulate— and deeply troubled. I knew by then the secret of good counseling: one must listen with the heart and give of oneself and of one's time. I tried hard to do just that. As time went on I seemed to discover a pattern in that girl's attitude and her words. I finally interrupted her: "Barbie," I said, feeling excited for no reason, "do you look on time as your enemy?"

She frowned. "Why do you ask that," she said. "What does it have to do with my problems?"

I shook my head. "Never mind, if you can't see any connection," I smiled, "just think about my question and answer it!"

Barbara thought for a while. "Yes," she said, "I *do* see time as my enemy in many ways. I just hate to think that I'll soon be thirty. I hate it that I have to work and give most of my time to a punch clock. I hate to sleep because I lose so much time when I could do fun things!"

I thought, "That is it! Most Americans fight with time as their greatest enemy—even the young people—but why?"

Barbara and I talked some more and when we parted we were both deep in thought. Barbara wondered how anyone could look at time as a friend—and I wondered the opposite. I have never thought of time as an enemy. Time had always seemed to be on my side, not against me.

One of my foster-mother's favorite sayings was: *"Es geht alles vorüber, Marichen, alles geht vorbei* [Everything passes, little Mary, everything comes to pass]." I had always been so glad for the truth of that saying. What if the Communist labor camp had been forever, or Nazi Germany, or childbirth, or a headache, or any of the many hardships which beset a human life? Certainly, good things pass, too—but time brings more good things with the bad. It's like rain and sunshine: it takes both to make things grow.

As for growing old, I had always been taught that it was life's crowning achievement. Age had wisdom, received deference, and as a child I had longed for that time when I would arrive at that honorable time of gray hair and maturity.

What was time, anyway? It started in its present human concept when sin and death began. God and the universe don't have a time-bound sense such as we do, God never changes—we humans do!

Well, if time was a result of sin, maybe the Americans did right to look at it as an enemy, I wondered. I prayed and searched the Bible and took time to do some deep thinking. I discovered that measured time existed before sin spoiled the picture. God made day and night as part of His Creation by putting different lights in the sky. He gave the earth a day-and-night cycle of twenty-four hours, before men measured time as we do—from birth to death. *All* men were given the same amount of time and God saw that it was good! And suddenly I understood America's rush for more time!

Americans have more of everything: food, material things, education, scientific knowledge, freedom, land—they are so used to it that they take it for granted. The only thing they share equally with the rest of the world is time. They cannot rent, hire, buy, or in any other way obtain more time. They cannot store it, freeze it, can it; it's perishable and cannot be brought back, ever. They cannot manufacture it, and time is perhaps the only *talent* that every human being is equally responsible for (*see* Matthew 25:15).

America has been able to split the atom, land on the moon, break the sound barrier, and subordinate matter and resources by superior scientific knowledge. Time and its limits, America cannot touch or change. It would seem, therefore, that time is regarded as an enemy to progress and the American way of life.

What a price we pay for this arrogance! Obsessed with a desire to stay forever young, we cannot look forward to the serenity and beauty of the sunset years. Worse yet, we barely even tap the great resources of wisdom and experience which come to us with age and time. Millions of America's aged are paying the price for their own fight with time by now being left behind by the young generation. It is also a well-known fact that successful Americans who think in time-and-number concepts are prone to heart attacks and similar diseases. Perhaps it's a new way of avoiding old age!

What about our mania for speed? Is it worthwhile to "win" time if we mutilate lives—even our own?

Most of all, can a child of God fight with time, and honor Him simultaneously as the Giver of our time? If the Kingdom of God is within us *now,* are we not fighting eternity in ourselves? Is not all our life based on time? Life is the greatest possession anyone has. Why fight life by fighting time?

God has a time for everything. If we learn to go by His timing, we shall have enough time on our hands—twenty-four hours every day, to be exact.

9

Freedom, Pigtails, and Politics

One word that Americans use very often is *freedom.* They also call it "liberty" or "the right to live as we wish" or "the pursuit of happiness" or "passing the buck" or even, "Get off my back, it's none of your business"—and a hundred other such meaningful terms. No other word has ever frightened and fascinated me as much as that word *freedom.* I sensed that there was more to it than I could see in the beginning. The word had a sacred, oracular sound to me; it made me feel excited—and very scared.

Today I understand why the American film *Born Free* gripped me so mysteriously—I watched it as often as I was given a chance. The film shows the story of Elsa, a lioness, who had been raised in captivity. One day her human parents saw themselves forced to either put her into a cage or to acclimatize her to her native environment and let her go—free! They loved her so much that they decided to force her into freedom.

Force it had to be, since Elsa was afraid of freedom. How well I understood! Everytime I watched that film I cried again when I saw the part where Elsa limps back to her human parents' truck after she had been left out in the African wilderness for several days and nights. Elsa didn't know how to react in her natural habitat. She didn't enjoy freedom, she suffered under it at first. Elsa was born to be free, but she didn't know it. That beautiful animal nearly died before she learned to exchange the security of loving bondage for the precarious greatness of a free life—but she did it! Would I be able to do the same?

Unquestioning obedience to authority and dictatorship had molded my thinking and behavior during my formative years. Since I had never tasted freedom I did not miss it. I knew as little of the limitations imposed on my thinking and behavior by authoritarianism as does a caged animal who never left her cage.

When I walked out of my cage and from that old propeller airplane onto American soil and its freedom, I first felt only one compulsive desire: to return to the former securities and safe restrictions of my upbringing. My first taste of freedom was bitter. It was freedom all right: freedom from socialized medicine, workmen's compensation, and health police to protect slum tenants from rats, dirt, and exploitation by an unscrupulous landlord. It was also freedom to move anywhere—and freedom to survive or to die while nobody seemed to care.

I shall never forget the panic I felt when my husband injured his hand only a few weeks after our landing in America. We had no money left. We did arrive with one hundred dollars in our pockets and it gave us just a tiny bit of security. After all, one hundred dollars was at that time four hundred German marks. In our thinking, that was a pretty big sum for a refugee German! We lost even that little cushion of security the very first day we arrived.

Our sponsor explained to my husband that he had advanced the money for our train tickets to the World Church Service which had chartered the plane for us. We were given to understand that this was a sacrifice on our sponsor's part because now that money would not draw interest for him until we could pay it back. My husband told me in German what was said. We looked at each other. Without another word, he pulled out the whole hundred dollars and placed it into our sponsor's hand. I held my breath. Would he take it? He knew that it was *all* we possessed. It seemed to be the most evident and natural matter of course to that man. He took the money, nodded, and looked very pleased. We felt just the opposite, but tried not to show our fears. We were left without one penny in a strange land, and we knew it. When, shortly afterwards, disaster struck and Rudy couldn't work, there was for the first time in our lives no sick allowance. It was something we had taken for granted up to this point.

While I picked strawberries, cleaned houses, and steam ironed for a cleaning establishment in the unaccustomed summer heat of Michigan, I watched my confusion deepen and my feet swell as they had never before in my life. How could an advanced, rich nation like America be so behind times and have no *Kranken-kassen* (socialized medicine)?

Why did the American health authorities permit slums, when on the other hand they insisted that the airlines couldn't even reuse a perfectly clean lunch box and so much good material had to be thrown into big garbage cans?

Why was the owner of the cleaning shop allowed to let me work in a room where the heat would rise to 110 degrees by afternoon and nobody forced him to improve my work conditions? He had a cooler in his office but none in my little stuffy, sticky room. I knew he underpaid me, demanded overtime without ever paying more, and he acted terribly insulted when I quit because I couldn't stand it any longer. However, he *did* let me go! Was there nowhere an authority to protect people like me?

My questions deepened after we had survived the "dumb year" of immigrants and I was able to speak and read a basic vocabulary of English. For a long time I had to read with my German-English dictionary close beside me but I read every free minute—I still do! Books helped me to feel myself into the American way of thinking, though I often couldn't understand why they thought as they did.

Books and magazines told me that Americans lived *by choice* without socialized medicine. It was part of their philosophy of freedom. I also learned that my "ruthless" cleaner-boss was part of the free-enterprise system; he was free to exploit me—and I was free to walk out on him anytime I felt I had enough of his unfair treatment. That was a new concept to us. My husband and I learned to walk in and out of jobs. We worked our way up into the American mainstream of life and to middle-class status, but still, many questions remained unanswered for a long time to come.

Why was freedom so important? What could it do for a person or a nation that made it so special?

One thing I noticed very soon. Americans seemed to carry an unbelievable tolerance toward extremes in their life-styles and I wondered if it was a result of their free thinking.

I will never forget when, shortly after arriving in Los Angeles, I observed, one cool fall morning, two American ladies walk across the street. One lady wore a fur coat and high heels, the other, hot pants and a bikini halter top. I held my breath and looked around. Would the police come and arrest that nearly naked woman? No! Nobody came and nobody even seemed to notice, except my husband. It was obvious that he enjoyed the looks of the hot pants more than the fur coat which I admired.

I could clearly see that American women didn't care for uniformity of outward appearance. They liked to be different. Well, what if I dared to be different, too? The California heat was so oppressive to my head. I had hair long enough to sit on, and I wore it in a big bun above the neckline. I suffered much from headaches, and my hair always felt so heavy. Should I dare to just braid it in two long pigtails and let it hang?

Back home I would have never even given it one thought—it simply would have been impossible to go against the usual custom. A married European woman couldn't run around like a pig-tailed schoolgirl! Did I *dare* to do so in America? I contemplated for several days. One broiling-hot fall day I got desperate enough to let my hair down and walk outside my house.

"What beautiful hair you have!" exclaimed my neighbor kindly, as soon as she saw me. I couldn't believe my ears and eyes. She actually didn't even frown at me. I smiled, relieved, and smiled a lot more for days and weeks to come. Americans simply liked my long pigtails. (That, however, was ten years before the hippies came up with the same hairy idea and made pigtails and/or beards a sign of a bloodless youth revolution.) Later I cut my hair off, but until that time my pigtails became a symbol to me. That harmless nonconformity was my first faltering step toward a new exhilarating experience with freedom. I didn't know that then. I just wondered why I felt so excited about my boldness instead of feeling guilty for being different.

Yes, Americans are tolerant, respect individual differences, and yet become disagreeable when they turn to politics. Nearly every American sees himself as a political expert. In the beginning, it scared me. For an unexplainable reason Americans appear to see it as their highest duty to criticize everyone they themselves vote into political (and other) office. They don't whisper about it either; they say it loudly, they print it in the newspapers—and they get away with it. They call it "constructive criticism" or "Archie Bunker" or "All in the Family" but they don't keep it in the family. They tell it to the whole wide world.

I had always believed that one must leave politics to the politicians; they were trained for it, and the common person in Europe sees himself as unfit to dabble with that more or less dirty but complicated business. In America the common people talk, argue and differ on almost anything, especially politics. They also seem to have a sure answer and solution for everything, sometimes even before they understand or know the problem. Washington is criticized or tolerated like the daily weather report. People almost seem to expect the opposite of what is forecast.

What astounded me most was that on the one side Americans would dare to differ ever so freely and openly with one another and with their government, while at the same time they never silenced their opposition by force. *Why?* I wondered. These Americans had something I couldn't lay my finger on. What was it?

What is it that makes Americans so permissive (my pigtails)—so fiery disagreeable (elections)—and willing to laugh at themselves (Archie Bunker) all at the same time?

The word for it didn't exist in my vocabulary until I came to America.

Americans call it "tolerance" or "Live and let live" or "Go ahead and give it a try." It really is more than a word, I found out: it is a conviction which grows out of freedom. It permits bikinis, slums, pigtails, campus riots, Peace Corps, sit-ins, community drives, Disneylands, and "Archie Bunker running for President." He might not win—but he could give it a try if he wanted to and if it was "his thing" to do. Nobody would stop him. Was that a weakness or a strength in a political system? Was that approach good or bad?

How could I know?

10

A Sweet Taste

Freedom and democracy. Good, bad, or indifferent, I had to come to grips with this ideology in order to be at peace with myself.

I was puzzling over symptoms, not causes, and I knew it. How does one go about understanding freedom? I couldn't do it by feelings: I had too many mixed emotions about the American life-style.

The first great flash about freedom came to me shortly before my family and I became American citizens. We had been in this country for seven years and knew we had to make a decision. America was home to our children. They spoke English without an accent—and mimicked mine for the fun of it. They considered America their homeland and loved it—so did we. We knew we lived a good life in spite of our rough start and felt deeply grateful. After a special family council and thoughtful prayer we applied for our new citizenship.

I thought of it as a matter of red tape and legal papers but it turned out to be much more. First we had to prepare and study for a citizenship test. That was my very first brush with American history and it left me more flustered than ever. European history is bad enough with all those long-winded kings and emperors— but, in America, presidents don't reign until they die. I had to remember a new name for every four or eight years of American history. What a blessing that the U.S.A. was only 180 years old! I hated to think what I'd have to remember if this country had started in ancient days.

How this nation began was another strange tale to me. Little did I know then that someday the story of America's beginning would give me the final insight to the meaning of America's freedom. When I read about it for the first time it left me deeply moved but without comprehension. I crammed dates and names and went to my examination with fear and trembling. I knew my inability to remember names and numbers only too well. Thanks to that unexplainable American attitude of sufferance, I passed, though I couldn't remember who the American president was when I entered the U.S.A. Too bad I wasn't asked about Abraham Lincoln. I took to that man from the start. I just had a hard time remembering what he wrote. Was it the Constitution, the Bill of Rights, or the Gettysburg Address? All three sounded the same to me.

Anyway, I congratulated myself that I had passed the hurdle when we were called back to that same office a few days later. The same examiner was there and he looked rather disturbed: "Your papers have been checked and the higher authorities are making an additional request. Because of your rather unusual political background we are supposed to do some additional interviews and your answers will be put on tape. . . ."

I was crushed. Would I have to go back and memorize more names attached to a donkey or elephant party? I just couldn't keep those English names in my head, except for George Washington. He was that lad who got whipped because he cut down a cherry tree. I felt so sorry for him that I remembered his name.

"Sir," I said anxiously, "do I have to study more history for those new interviews?"

The official smiled. "Don't worry, Mrs. Hirschmann, there will be only present-day issues discussed and taped. You will be asked why you want to become a U.S. citizen; I know that much for sure!"

The question hooked into me and I tried to find an honest answer to it. I thought about it for days. . . . Was it for the good life? For too much food and the bulging closets? For the free education available to our children and ourselves? Or was it for the American freedom which I still didn't fully understand at that moment.

Papa helped me to see why I wanted to become an American citizen by a letter which arrived just at the right time for me. It was a daring letter, written in Czechoslovakia and if it had been censored by the Communists, Papa might have gone to prison for it. He had found Christ and a new family in his old age and we were writing frequently to each other. He wrote in that letter:

> *Marichen,* don't ever forget that God has favored you and your family in a special way. You are permitted to live in paradise already on this earth, and once in a while we catch a small glimpse of your good life through your letters. I don't envy you for your material prosperity, though I long sometimes to be able to give our two children better food and warmer clothing. But you live in paradise because you're free! You are free to serve God and train your children as you wish. I can't.
>
> The other day my Rudy came home from school and seemed upset. I sat at the window and he came over to me and said, "Papa, teacher said there is no God. The Russian astronauts have looked around in space and can find no trace of him." Oh, *Marichen,* do I need to tell you how I ache in my olden days to see my children be turned against God by godless teachers? Guess what my smart Rudy said to me? He looked out and up into the sky and said, "Papa, won't my teacher be surprised when she will see Jesus come back again?" *Marichen,* what shall I do? How do I protect my children in the future? We have no children's books for them, no pictures. *Marichen,* sometimes I am afraid that I shall not make it into the kingdom of God after all. You see, I can't overcome my hate toward the Communists. I hate them for trying to steal my children's hearts. But my Bible says that I must love my enemies and pray for my government. I can't.

I put my head on that letter and sobbed. "Lord," I cried, "help my people!"

A few days later I sat across from the American immigration official. He asked me only one question: "Why do you want to become an American citizen?" I looked down at a microphone and said, "Because this country gives me freedom to worship God according to my conscience, it lets me be free. . . ."

Freedom began to taste sweet to me and I knew it. With the new

U.S. citizenship I felt a greater responsibility to get involved and to defend my new homeland whenever I heard people tear it down. I shall never forget what one teacher answered me, after I had enrolled in an American college and took a political-science class. I said to him: "If I had my way, I would pass a law that the American press would have to print at least 50 percent good things about America. All they do now is report the bad things. What will the rest of the world think of America? They have no other way to see America but through the eyes of the news media, and what a distorted reflection they get. America is more than what the news says."

I knew I was blazing with righteous indignation: that's how furious I felt! Someone had just shared with us an editorial which had not *one* good word to say about the American government.

The teacher nodded and smiled that typical American tolerant smile. "I agree with you, Maria," he said warmly. "I wish the press would be less negative, too—but I am willing to lay down my life to stop you from passing a law to force the press to be more positive. The moment you start forcing people to do *your* ideal thing, you destroy freedom."

I stared into his eyes. Was he for real? Yes, he was. And I was too overwhelmed to say another word. It was obvious that I simply couldn't follow the American way of thinking. Every time I thought I had found the answer I discovered that I had one of two things in my mouth: a sweet taste—or my foot. Which was it?

11

Give Me Freedom!

Some years went by. With two college degrees and experience in teaching high-school dropouts, one Sunday morning I found myself in a prison chapel ready to speak to young prisoners.

At that time the American prisons were peopled with militants, rioters, and other young persons who felt they must change their country by force. I had been warned that the chapel was half-filled with these elements and that they might break up the worship service if I said the wrong thing.

I felt weary and torn inside. I knew I loved God and America. I believed in freedom and democracy but how could I defend it when there was so much poverty, injustice, and now all those campus riots and the violence everywhere? The issue of freedom troubled me again. I prayed for wisdom, and gave my testimony for God and America to those young prisoners. Nobody broke up the meeting and I received a standing ovation at the end—but not from everyone! Some of those fellows just sat and stared at me.

One of them stood up after everything had quieted down and challenged me: "Since you think America is so great," he said and glared at me, "what do you think about us young people of America and our attempts to improve this country? What do you think about the protest marches and riots?" I saw his face break into a crafty smile and I knew that one wrong word of mine could start the expected riot.

It happened again that morning. A flash hit me: some new insights were born. After months of brooding and wondering, I saw a new dimension in place of single puzzles.

"My friend," I said with a new conviction, "young people are the same all over this globe. They long for a challenge and a task in which to measure their strength. I have come from a country where young people feel as you do, but the only way they can protest is to throw themselves before a Russian tank. And the tank doesn't stop! Or they can pour gasoline over themselves (if they have a ration card for it) and then ignite it—and they had better burn fast or the authorities stop the suicide and heal the fellows to give them a trial and sentence of death! Yes, I am aware that American people are afraid of your riots and protests, but I am not. I watch these happenings on the TV news and all I can feel is astonishment—yes, even gratefulness, that I am permitted to live in a country that is so free that it *lets* you riot as much as you do. I only wish American young people would do it a bit nicer!

"My young friends, I have long searched for the meaning of democracy and freedom. I thought Americans knew it, but they don't. Americans are the ones who seem to know the least about the value and philosophy of the freedom they possess. Listen, you fellows: freedom makes good people better and bad people worse. Remember that! Some of the rough things happening in America today are the price this land pays for its freedom. As for me, I prefer to pay the price and stay in this land. Those who can't take it should find another land; they might be happy to come back to these United States after a short time in another country!"

I sat down. There was no riot after I had spoken. It was so quiet in the chapel, we could have heard a needle drop. The prisoners either filed out in silence or they came to shake my hand before I left.

Metal doors opened and closed behind me and I walked back to my car, to sunshine and to freedom. I felt so jubilant that I didn't know what to do with myself. My soul's window had opened and the longer I looked out the more beauty I discovered.

I suddenly began to understand why one couldn't pass a law to force the American press to be positive and why Americans hesitate to crush their riots and protests by outer control. They know instinctively that outer control destroys freedom. I understood what outer control could do since I had lived under it most of my life. Now, for the first time, I saw the other side of the coin. Freedom operates by inner control and Americans seem to have a deep trust in it. I wondered: What is that inner control? Where did the Americans get it? Why do they trust it so much that they can be as tolerant and permissive as they are? How did it start? I stood at the brink of new discoveries and my excitement mounted. Where did the American concept of freedom begin?

For the first time since my Nazi training I began to have an interest in history again. History had been my favorite subject in Nazi school but I turned against it when Nazi Germany died. History was a lie, I had concluded, for Hitler used history as a tool to brainwash us. Ever since the German collapse I was afraid of history in any form or description. Even in America I ended up with a humiliating *C* grade in U.S. History because of this fear.

Now, years later, without the pressure of those ghastly multiple-choice tests on my mind, I dug out books and went back to the beginning of this nation.

It seems to me that for most Americans the fact and the meaning of the *Mayflower* and the New England colonies is so well known as to be commonplace; scarcely worthy of a thought. Furthermore, they appear to know so little about world history and the rise and fall of other nations that they have no comparison nor comprehension of how much American history differs from any other national history in this world.

World history has one thread and theme: wars and power struggles to gain or regain more power. Nations are born and die according to their military strength. The stronger conquers the weaker and then is free to force. *Powerful outer forces bring order and control.* That concept seemed as natural to my thinking as is the law of gravity.

I had never before heard of any nation that started with a handful of defenseless people who left everything behind so that they might have freedom. Freedom for what? To conquer? To find riches and to raid as Columbus did when he set out to discover India and landed in the New World? Hitler and the Nazis used the word *freedom* incessantly to build the German Reich. More than one hundred and forty million young people are right now marching under the red banner of Communism. They call it "freedom."

What motive, what meaning lay in the freedom that cradled America? The freedom to worship God according to one's conscience— every American knows that by heart.

I found God and freedom so completely intertwined in America's early history that it overwhelmed me. How was that possible? People from everywhere in the world made up young America's ever-growing population. They had as many opinions and different backgrounds as can be imagined—nevertheless, the American freedom concept remained constant. Who set America's foundation and public opinion so firmly that even today it influences our nation's thinking?

America's concepts were cradled and formed in its church pulpits. America's preachers and Christian orators coined America's freedom, and humble teachers in little crude schoolhouses taught, from the Bible, freedom's deepest meaning.

Now I understood why America's freedom was built on *inner control*. The Christian God does not work by outer constraint. He works only as an inner power based on freedom of choice. As soon as I understood that, I understood also America's attitude toward individualism. Inner control can *never* be imposed on masses. Freedom of choice and conscience is an individual matter and therefore America's freedom stands and falls with every individual citizen.

When the full impact of that thought hit me, I felt dizzy again. I had grown up with the idea that the individual amounted to nothing. People were important in Nazi Germany, but only as a part of the nation that was everything. Every human value, virtue and desire had to serve *dem Volk* (multitudes, masses). The whole was always more than its individual parts. The part's highest fulfillment was to sacrifice itself for the whole. With that deeply ingrained attitude I had read American human-interest stories and puzzled. I never forgot one story I found in the *Reader's Digest*. It told about a family who had lost a little retarded boy in the woods while camping. They asked the community for help. Several thousand Americans showed up and combed the area for several days. The little boy was found and everybody went home with tears of rejoicing. I read and reread the article many times.

Why did American people give so much of their time and strength to save *one* little retarded child? It wasn't that I disagreed—if I had been around I would have helped, too. I just couldn't understand what motivated those people so deeply.

I still remember when the German papers had printed a story about a little baby in Hamburg. She needed bananas in order to survive some strange disease. American soldiers found out about it. There were no bananas in those harsh, hungry German postwar days. The GI's flew bananas in for several months at their own expense to save that child; and the German newspapers flipped over it. So did I! Why would anyone do such a costly thing to save *one* child?

Now I understood. I saw the reason for it and I saw myself and my place in the American society in a new light. I even saw myself with new eyes. All my life I had felt guilty for being "just me." I tried ever so hard to lean, depend, obey, and conform to outer power. Now I understood why I had such a hard time with it. I wasn't created that way. I was "born free" like Elsa, the lioness, but for too long I had not known it.

I have often thought about Elsa since I last saw the film. Would Elsa ever have been willing and able to go back to human bondage and her "security" after she had learned to love freedom? I don't know how lions feel and think, but I know what living under freedom has done for me. I know at last who I am and where I stand.

America! Give me the bitter with the sweet—my own individual responsibility for my behavior—the scary thought that I, as an individual, have a part in America's destiny by my inner control and choice.

America! Give me tolerance towards the imperfections of democratic governments and its extremes.

Give me freedom under God—or give me death!

12

What Is Creativity?

Creativity. There was a time not so many years ago when this word was not even in my vocabulary.

To know freedom is to understand life, God, love, creativity, and other great human concepts in a totally new dimension. At least, that is what happened to me when I began to see the inner power of freedom under God. For instance, I had wondered for many years what Americans meant when they used the word *creativity.* What does creativity mean? The word didn't even exist for me before I came to America. Thinking back, I believe that I equated *rebellion* with being creative. The way I always had to fight my unruly spirit made me feel guilty and eager to get it out of my system.

I shall never forget the moment when the word *creativity* came to my attention for the very first time. The first few years of struggle for survival in the United States had passed, and I found myself a bit bored. The children were past the diaper stage and I felt eager to get out of the house once in a while.

The city we lived in at the time offered evening courses in adult education at their City College. Those classes were within my reach. Not sure if I could yet handle the English language, I decided to play it safe and start out with an art course. I enrolled in watercoloring. I felt rather smart about my choice since I had had art training in Nazi school and watercolors were one of my favorite mediums. Still, nearly twenty years had gone by since I had last touched a watercolor brush.

It was my first contact with American adult education and I walked into the classroom with a lot of nervous butterflies in my stomach. The teacher was an elderly, bony spinster who eyed all of us over the rims of her thick glasses. The first thing we had to do was introduce ourselves. My accent caught everyone's attention and questions began to fly. "Where are you from?" "How long have you lived in the States?" "How do you like it in America?"

So far, so good. I was used to answering such questions. Then the teacher asked, "Mrs. Hirschmann, what school did you attend in Europe?"

I bit my lips and squirmed into a long silence. If there was one thing I didn't want to tell, it was that I had been trained in a special Nazi school. But as a Christian, I couldn't lie, so I stuttered my "confession" and wondered what would happen next. The teacher's face turned a shade more sour, but she didn't say anything and I felt relieved.

The class began and we were supposed to start with finger painting to "loosen up"—I had never heard of such a thing and waited to see. What could *finger painting* be? I had never used my fingers to paint in my former German classes. I watched. Soon I knew—and I couldn't believe my eyes. The waste of paper, paint, and starch overwhelmed me. Hesitatingly I reached for some materials. It looked like fun, but I was determined not to be as wasteful as the others, and please my teacher.

Slowly and ever so carefully, I began my one and only masterpiece. I was painting a sunset and tried hard to make it look real and keep my hands clean at the same time. The teacher came and looked over my shoulders. I straightened, turned, and smiled into her face. Her eyes bore into me like cold steel and after a short glance at my work she said, loud enough that everyone could hear it: "That Adolf Hitler surely ruined every bit of creativity in you!" With that she walked off.

If she had slapped me in the face, it couldn't have hurt more. My smile froze and tears pushed into my eyes. I bent over my paper and fought for composure. As soon as I could, I leaned toward the next art student so I could see what I was doing that was so terribly wrong. She was a pleasingly plump woman about my age who was up to her elbows in paint and who obviously was having fun covering paper after paper with the wildest designs.

"Ma'am," I said politely, "what did the teacher mean, please? I do not understand her words."

The woman gave me a warm, reassuring smile. "Never mind that old sourpuss. What she means to say is that you mustn't be so careful. Just feel free to experiment. See. . . ." And she pointed to her many papers.

I nodded and was more confused than ever. First of all, how did she dare to call a teacher a sourpuss? (I had labeled her "sour" in my *mind,* but that was different.) Couldn't a student be expelled from class for such disrespect? Next I wondered why I *should* experiment. That just wasted expensive material and teacher might get more upset with me. Most of all, what was *creativity* and why and how did Hitler ruin it in me?

I soon found the answer to the first two questions. It was only a matter of a few more classes before I caught on to the swing of things. I learned not to be afraid of the teacher, to "waste" material, and to experiment freely while feeling only moderately guilty—and I dragged a lot of paintings home. My teacher and I even became friends before the course was over. We found out that both of us loved cats and that drew us together. I received an *A* from her and I popped with delight. But still, I could not forget that remark of hers; it stuck like an arrow in my soul.

What was *creativity?* When my dream of dreams came true just a few years later and I was able to attend an American college full-time to get my degrees in teaching and counseling, I gave that matter renewed attention. I read books on the creative child and came to the conclusion that I must have been one of those youngsters. At least I qualified by the troubles I had been in during my younger years.

It was me, all right: a child who always tried to solve problems the unusual way, a child who was laughed at because she came up with crazy thoughts, a child who was punished often and harshly because she had a hard time conforming without asking a hundred times,

"Why, but why?" I had never been able to accept authority just because someone said so! I would challenge it and take the punishment rather than keeping quiet.

My mother would look at me and say: "Why can't you be like Anni or Gustl?" (my foster-sisters). What she didn't know was that I tried hard to be a model child to please her, but I couldn't. The harder I tried, the more difficult it got, and I would often feel so discouraged with myself and life in general that I just wouldn't try any longer. Americans have a special term for children such as I was. They call it the "black sheep" and wherever there is one, whether it be at home or church, people have a lot to say about it. It isn't all kind, either.

Hitler finally tamed my searching spirit, clipped my wings, and Nazi school helped me to learn how to conform and fit. I tried to stay that way even after Nazism was gone. I simply thought it a virtue to obey in thought and action, and conform at all cost.

And . . . along comes my very first American teacher and "slaps" me for it.

Well, my study in psychology gave me some ideas about creativity but it was all very elusive. Since it can't be measured scientifically, creativity is still rather hard to define. Of course, there is always that popular opinion that artistic people are creative. It just bothered me to think that creativity was a rare handout to a few special human beings who could paint, compose music, or write poetry. It didn't seem fair; nor could I believe that some of the modern art had anything to do with creativity. It was not until I understood the concept of the individual's freedom of choice that I found my answer. God is the Creator. He created and creates still. His Spirit and Word created the earth, mankind, the universe. In every rebirth of conversion, He creates a new heart and a new spirit.

The Bible tells us that man was made in God's likeness, therefore every human being should have some creative forces in himself akin to his Creator.

Does that mean that everyone should be able to paint, compose, or write?

No, a child of God has creative forces available in his every human ability, in every thought and action, which might include artistic tendencies. But artistic abilities are not a prerequisite to being creative. I believe today that creativity begins in my thinking. How? By seeing myself, first of all, as someone who has freedom of choice. Americans will say, "What is so special about that? Of course, I see myself free to make my own choices. That's to be taken for granted."

No, it doesn't need to be taken for granted. I see it as a great privilege and I waited a long time to make that exciting discovery. Most people on this globe don't know that there is individual freedom and freedom of choice and that it was designed by God for mankind. Americans know it, for we *are* free.

How free are we? Are we really free to think creatively by our own choice and will? How conditioned are we? How much are even Americans shaped, driven, and forced by circumstances, time, culture, roles, and the "class" we belong to? How often do we say: "I just can't help it. I simply *have* to explode, crave, dislike, because. . . ."

Whenever we cannot help ourselves, we certainly don't have freedom of choice! Whenever fate or environment manipulates us, we are not free, but robots who are at the mercy of luck and misfortune.

I have observed many unfree people in my *free* new homeland, America, and it bothers me deeply. Unless my free fellow Americans learn to understand the value, meaning, and the implication of creative freedom we might lose it someday—for good.

That frightening fact came home to me when I read an article in the local newspaper about an interview between a news reporter and Dr. B.F. Skinner, a psychology professor at Harvard University. That learned man sees everything and everybody as a result of conditioning. In his eyes, people are like rats who can be conditioned to run a complex maze, open little gates to catch some food, or avoid painful stimuli by pushing certain buttons. Human beings are nothing more than the sum of preshaped outer and inner conditioning forces.

In other words, he sees even us Americans as lacking a free will. We all behave and act according to our upbringing and the way our stomach juices and other parts of us react to our environment. Skinner sees a time when behavioral scientists will be able to control *any* individual's behavior completely. Freedom of choice is totally outdated in Skinner's eyes. He believes that the whole earth in its present condition needs total control. He sees even himself as a puppet without a choice.

Skinner forgot to tell in that interview *who* he feels will control the controllers of humanity someday. I personally can't help but wonder (and worry) if he plans to be one of them.

Americans tolerate such theories as very farfetched and way-out. I don't. I am too much aware of the fact that the largest part of humanity on this globe is already under a "big brother's" control. I was, too, and how it crippled my thinking for much too long!

How free are we really? Do Americans *want* their individual creative freedom? It takes courage to accept the responsibility for *all* our thinking and doing. In other words, our own choice creates not only our inner self, but to a certain degree even our environment. "As a man thinketh in his heart, so is he" (*see* Proverbs 23:7). A man thinks free, he *is* free; a man thinks creatively, he *is* creative. It works the other way around, too.

If that holds true, *I* decide, for instance, how my days go! When I get up in the morning I might feel miserable. Since feelings cannot be turned off or on by will, I have to turn to my freedom of choice and to my willpower. I either can grumble, "Oh-h-h, is it morning?" or I can say, "Good morning, dear Lord. Thank You for giving me another day."

Whatever I decide at that moment will not only create my own attitudes for that day but also the moods for other people. I dare to say that in many a "free" American home the mornings would be different if the positive, creative freedom of choice was understood and applied. It might even cause some faintings, but not by the one who decided to create something *good,* for a change.

Human beings are *free* to create smiles, laughter, special days for the family and other people—glad surprises, new ways of doing the same old thing, goodwill and a hundred other worthwhile possibilities—and it all starts in our thinking and with our own creative will. Oh, how I thank God that I am free to be creative!

13

What About Evil?

The mystery of evil? Even before the days of Job, the classic sufferer, "What to do with the bad things in life which are not under our control," is a question that has absorbed humanity. Does freedom end when sickness strikes—when poverty limits—when the other person is cruel and inhuman?

Even after I understood that I had creative powers to think and to do the good, I didn't know what to do with the bad. I also wondered how fair it was that most people on the globe could never taste freedom and discover all those deep dimensions about life. It was a Jew, Dr. Viktor Frankl, a famous Austrian psychiatrist, who showed me the place of creativity in suffering and adversity. Dr. Frankl does not claim to be a Christian; he sees himself as an existentialist. He spent long years in a Nazi concentration camp in Germany. For many years I didn't have the courage to read his books. In his book *Man's Search for Meaning* he tells how his persecutors took everything from him: his family, his clothing, his manuscript which was a result of his lifework—and his human dignity. He watched others throw themselves into the electric wire to end it all: the misery, the hunger, the cruelties, the meaninglessness of life.

Viktor Frankl made himself a firm promise not to "run into the wire" because he knew something that most of the others there in the concentration camp apparently didn't know. He knew that after every other value as a human being had been taken away from him, there was one value left which nobody could ever take. His own attitude. And it was that attitudinal value which set him free. Even in a concentration camp!

It was during, and partly *because of* these almost incredible sufferings and degradations that he began to create and develop his theories on Logotherapy. Today thousands, perhaps millions of people have found a new meaning for their lives because of that new therapy.

I personally believe that a loving God gave Frankl the strength to hold out as long as he did, for the world needed what Dr. Frankl created, *in suffering,* to give to us. And nobody else could have given us these discoveries except a man as creative as he is.

Viktor Frankl is the first one who would tell you that in order to be truly human, a person must be creative. And that even in the face of overwhelming forces like incurable sickness, injustice, or death, there is a meaning: a personal meaning created by the right way of thinking. Every individual has to find his *own* meaning for every aspect of life.

Whenever God creates, there is life. Whenever a person changes *from* reacting *to* creative thinking and acting, he changes *from* mere existing *to* the abundant life. Or, as Dr. Frankl puts it, he develops toward "true morality" in being a human.

Thinking back to that precious spinster-teacher who tried so hard to make a good watercolor artist out of me, I am afraid she never quite succeeded in making me a famous painter. Maybe great art works are not our greatest need at the present, anyway!

The present times need people who create—by their thinking and doing—a living example to follow. An example that will lead other humans from mere existing to living, from rat cages to freedom, from creativeness to their Creator.

We Americans will likely never have to face the horrors which Dr. Frankl suffered, but is that an excuse to ignore the creative forces of our mind? Do we have a right to let our attitudes deteriorate just because ours is a simple, uneventful, humdrum life which frustrates our wants? If the free, average American has a hard time putting creativity and positive freedom of choice into his daily, wearisome existence it might be because he doesn't know better—but what about us Christians?

We should know better! The Holy Word of God is full of admonition on how to think right, how to give praise even in hardship, and it gives us examples of people who created victories out of defeat by their thinking—among them Daniel and Joseph.

Our greatest example is the Lord Jesus Christ. He, the Creator of the universe and our earth, came to us as a human being. By His choice, He accepted the limitations and hereditary weaknesses of the human race. He claimed no more than we can claim: He had nothing more to work with and to live by than we can have. He used His human creativity to preach, teach and heal, to bring joy, peace, and blessings to others, and at last to die by His own free choice. The Romans captured His body, some of the Jews spat in His face, but nobody and nothing ever overpowered His *mind,* His *spirit,* and His *love.* Jesus Christ created His own free environment by His thinking, even at the cross—and so can we.

Don't we all know of people who triumphed over poverty, sickness, and death? We do, but we always think of them as special people. We see them as spiritual giants whom we admire, but we would never dare to put ourselves on their level. But we all may know this triumph: it is actually an essential to our final Christian maturity. By it we do not only glorify, but defend our Creator-God. He longs to be defended by us: His common, average, creative human beings which He Himself created. How can we do this? Where do we start? By praising Him! For what? *For everything!* "In all things give thanks," God tells us (*see* 1 Thessalonians 5:18). Why? I admit that I knew *how* to give thanks—even for hardships—long before I understood *why.* But I did find out!

Very often, when I can't understand something, I go to the beginning. Just as I learned to comprehend America's freedom concept by studying its early history, so was I led by God's Spirit to the beginning of Creation and humanity to grasp the full meaning of human praise to God, even in suffering.

Suffering, according to the Bible, did not start in the Garden of Eden: it began in heaven. It began with a beautiful angelic being named Lucifer. When God, the Creator, made that "glorious son of the morning" (*see* Isaiah 14:12) as one of the countless beings and angels He created all over the universe, evil and hurt did not exist as a reality. It only existed as a possibility. The possibility of evil existed before its reality. This had to be so, otherwise there could have been no freedom of choice—and love always gives a choice: it never forces loyalty. God took a risk every time He created any creature with a free choice to turn against Him. His angels in heaven had that choice—and one third of the angelic host turned against their Creator when evil changed from a possibility to tangible rebellion. It put war into heaven and the Creator-God on trial. Yes, God has been on trial before His created universe ever since Lucifer became Satan and the possibility of evil given by a God of love became horrible reality. God could have avoided all of that by creating robots and by conditioning them into a prescribed behavior pattern, but God is love and the principles of love are based on freedom of choice. Anything less would have degraded God's character and His universal rulership.

I do not know of what Satan accused God, in heaven. He was convincing enough, though, that one third of the heavenly host followed that deceiver. But I do know why God is on trial on our earth. In the Garden of Eden, God was accused of being a liar; today He is despised and blasphemed by some of His human creatures as unfair, jealous, hard, revengeful, unjust—and the great controversy which began in heaven is going on as a "theater" for the whole universe to behold on our little planet, even today.

Why does God permit this? Because love gives freedom of choice. God *is* love and His love made a painful choice long before man ever did. The Lamb of God—Jesus Christ—was slain, in the mind of God, before the foundation of this earth was laid. When love permitted the possibility of sin it had to provide at the same moment the remedy for sin. Love provided the best which heaven had to give. Sin became a reality and God did not destroy Satan and evil as He could have; He permitted Satan full display before the entire universe.

I often wondered why—if evil had been wiped out in the beginning, the earth would not have had to become a showplace for the devil, and we humans would not have to suffer and die as we all must.

God's fairness had to permit evil to ripen in order to give the universe time to observe and make a free choice for or against Him. If evil had received its just punishment immediately, God would have been served in fear by all His creatures from that moment on—and love cannot exist that way; it would rather go on a *cross!*

Yes, God chose to let Himself be put on trial after He assumed the full responsibility, and He paid the whole penalty Himself. An entire universe witnessed the conflict and could decide, once and for all, who is just and right. However, we humans are still caught in the middle of the conflict. Is that fair? No, there is absolutely nothing fair about the whole matter and God could be the first one to complain about it. He was treated the least fair in that deal. He ended up on a cross because He dared to love so much that He gave His creatures freedom of choice. He suffered, agonized—and died—and never complained—never defended Himself.

He still doesn't. The trial is not yet over. Man is still shaking his fist in God's face blaming Him for sin and suffering. Satan is still going around like a roaring lion trying to snatch souls away from Jesus. God owns men twice: once by creation and second by redemption. But He still gives what love always gave—*freedom of choice.*

Isn't there anyone who defends God in that unfair trial? His angels long to do it but God permits it not. The *only* beings who are permitted to defend God are *human* beings. Humans are not only part of the drama and conflict, humans are akin to their Creator, made in His image, able to create by choice.

We create trial or defense for God by every choice we make, by every word we say. We show His love when we praise Him for His blessings and goodness, but it is as we *triumph* over suffering and evil that we defend God's righteousness and expose Satan as the originator of all sin and suffering.

To praise God as long as we have nothing to complain about is nothing more than human decency. To praise God in the face of incurable sickness, injustice, evil, and death puts human creativity back to its divine beginning. For God, who *is* love and creativity, overflowed with both. So much so that He needed a channel, an expression of Himself—and He made you and me.

14

To Make Love

Every nation and every era has its particular words and phrases; often, through overuse, they are in danger of becoming clichés. Nazi Germany's *Ehre* (honor) and *Treue* (loyalty) were emphasized to such an extent that they greatly crippled my understanding of other words and their values.

One word I heard to excess in America was a word that had never attracted my attention before. It was *love.* Germans don't use the word *love* too freely—and the term *to make love* just does not exist in the German language (or mind).

Love was like freedom: I felt drawn to it, but it also scared me. Love equaled big emotions in my thinking, and I was afraid of emotionalism in any shape or form. Emotionalism had brainwashed me into becoming a Nazi. Anything that smacked of emotionalism made me feel defensive and uneasy. I knew I didn't understand too much about love, but I couldn't help thinking about it.

How little I knew about the unlimited scope of love came home to me shortly after we had arrived in America. We had moved out of our rat-infested slum apartment into a clean, warm basement and I was slowly tuning into life again. Our social life was far from fancy, of course, but we had several very dear friends by then. One of them was *Tante* Erhard—a Russian-German immigrant whose husband had been sent away to a Communist labor camp in Siberia and was never seen again. She had emigrated to America with her two small sons years before we did and she was already more settled and acquainted with the American way of life. She was also a brave little woman who scrubbed toilets, floors, houses, and offices to provide for her two boys. Her courage inspired me and her wisdom guided me through greenhorn confusion and much inexperience. She became my confidante, a mother substitute, and a shoulder to cry on. I respected her advice because I trusted her.

We ate many meals in her house and my children loved to go to her humble apartment. She had watched me nag at my children while we had dinner together. I was determined to teach my two children *German* table manners and not let them eat the American way. To me, at that time, Americans ate like barbarians. They didn't even use their knives consistently, but only to cut up the food. Then, with their left hands in their laps, they would slouch over and gobble up the food. *How uncultured,* I sneered inwardly. *We Hirschmanns might be poor, but we would never be so-ooo uncivilized! Tante* Erhard's boys did eat the American way already, and my children were copying them. So, with a frown, I commanded my children, "Take your fork in your left hand and your knife in your right," and I made it sound as if their whole future depended on their observing this custom. It didn't, I found out later.

Christel, my seven-year-old, a quiet, easygoing girl, had a streak of defiance in her face.

"If you don't obey Mommy," I said sternly, "I won't love you anymore."

Christel obeyed and I was pleased. After the meal the children played and I helped *Tante* Erhard wash dishes. My motherly friend looked up as soon as nobody else could hear us and said, "Marianne, you must never, ever, again say to your children what you said at the table!"

"What did I say?" I asked innocently. I had no idea what she meant.

"That you wouldn't love your children anymore, if they disobeyed or did wrong! My dear, we love our children regardless of how they behave!"

I stared into her tired, aged, gentle face and swallowed hard. I didn't know if I should feel embarrassed or surprised. Wasn't love something that had to be earned by good behavior? Wasn't love a cause-effect relationship?

Nobody had ever told me that I was loved until I began dating, but

I was told from babyhood on when I was *not* loved. Whenever I did something that displeased someone I heard: *"Ich mag dich nicht mehr* [I don't like you anymore]." Most of the time I was not liked and I knew it.

When I did right I did only what was expected of me—it deserved no comment. I remembered how much I had longed as a child to hear sometimes: *"Ich mag dich* [I like you]"—but nobody ever said it, not even Mother. My society used words sparingly and love was to be guessed, not expressed.

I had made a deliberate effort to express love verbally to my own children. Whenever they were good I told them that I loved them. I didn't want them to grow up as love-starved as I had been. They shouldn't have to guess that they were loved whenever they tried to do right.

I began to ponder: *Was love more than a reward? Tante* Erhard's words touched my innermost soul, and I left her place that evening deep in thought and in search of new horizons. I have never again said to my children or anyone else what I said that night at the dinner table. *Tante* Erhard was right. I could sense that and I obeyed her immediately. It took me much longer to understand all that she meant by it.

What was love? A big feeling? I had thought so, ever since I had become a teenager and witnessed in myself and others the deep surge of physical and emotional attachment to certain people of the other sex. Love was sentimental, romantic, poetic—and fickle! One day I felt myself in love; the next day the feeling was gone. My love was as unstable as my feelings, which depended on the weather, how much sleep and food I got, and what my body chemistry was like.

The same held true after I got married and became a mother. When I felt right, I loved my family; when I got angry or irritated, I didn't love them. I spanked and yelled instead. Or did I love even when I punished? The Bible said that God does both. "Whom God loveth, him he also chasteneth" (*see* Hebrews 12:6). That was hard to understand and it didn't make sense, but I accepted it.

I do not remember if someone said this to me or if I read it: "Love is not a feeling. Love is a principle. Feeling is to love what salt is to soup. It gives it a better flavor but it is not the soup itself."

Love is a principle! How does a principle work? By our reasoning and willpower! I knew that much before I went back to college and studied psychology. Through my studies I gained new insight into human behavior and the importance of the human will. We love others with our will first and let feelings fall into place, if so possible. Now I understood in retrospect why Jesus had shown me, even before I came to America, that I must pray for my enemies regardless of how I felt about them.

Yes, I had prayed for years for the Russian who had raped my best girl friend and for that Czech overseer who had treated us so very inhumanely in labor camp. My feelings about those men, however, had never changed though I had obeyed God and prayed. I felt guilty about feeling so resentful and I tried to change my emotions—it never worked.

Not until I studied it deeply did I learn to accept the fact that we humans are not in command of our emotions. All we can create are favorable environments, set by our will. What a relief! I finally understood how to love! Wasn't that great? But whenever we think we have arrived, we find there is more to learn.

It was not until I caught the meaning of freedom and the importance of the individual in the eyes of democracy and of God, that I finally understood a completely new concept in the realm of love.

The Bible says that we must love our neighbor as ourselves. To love *myself*? That I had never dared to do. I tried ever so hard to love others, to be less demanding (even to the extent that my children were finally permitted to eat and act the American way), but I was merciless with myself. I demanded perfection of myself and never attained it, therefore my will and I were at war with each other at all times. I could never please myself and I knew it. I frequently drove myself into complete exhaustion and felt right about it, for I deserved it!

Even after I had found Christ as my Saviour, I had never seen myself as an individual, but as a part of a whole—the church. When I finally understood that I was an individual in my own right, that there was only one of me on the whole wide globe and I had a *right* to be me, it was nearly too much to comprehend.

The greatest adventure besides discovering God and America was when He taught me to discover myself. God taught me that He loved me because I was His unique creation and different from anyone else, not in spite of it. He was honored by my difference, and I could stop feeling guilty for being me. God specializes in differences, not in "making alike"—whatever He creates is unique. No two snowflakes or leaves are ever reproduced the same by our Creator; love respects and creates originals, not carbon copies.

Whenever man is not in harmony with God, he tries to force alikeness. Communism, Nazism, materialism, church legalism—any environment without Christ's principles will fight differences and glorify uniformity. It will induce guilt in a person for wanting to be what God gave to humans as one of His greatest gifts. Yes, God delights in everybody's uniqueness. He is in love with *me* in a different way than with anyone else, because there was nobody exactly like me, ever, and there will never be anyone like me. Because God is in love with *me,* I can do the same: I can love myself.

It is one thing to fall in love with others, but what a special time I had when I began to make peace with myself. Everything fell into place: the Bible texts which say that God does not condemn us even if our own hearts do, and that God loves us even if we don't love Him. I had puzzled over that for a long time. Psychology had taught me that *any* human love was based on trust. We react to love as long as we are not afraid and we are able to trust.

God's love has to be greater and different if He can love us *before* He can trust us. He doesn't *react* to us, He acts in His love. The Creator loves us unconditionally—His love does not depend on our response. He is in love with every creature's uniqueness: even mine. The thought still makes me dizzy and I feel overwhelmed—like Paul: *Oh, what depth of love!* (*See* Ephesians 3:18.)

What a new responsibility I saw for me after I saw myself with

God's eyes. I was no longer permitted to drive myself without mercy. I had to give my body and soul rest, relaxation, and permission to enjoy life. I even had to accept the humanness of making mistakes without punishing myself over and over for it. I also saw that I had a calling nobody else has, or ever had, or ever will have. If I don't fulfill that calling, someone else has to do what I was supposed to do. But nobody else will be able to do it as uniquely as I could have done it if I stayed in tune with God.

The more I learned to love myself, the more I learned to love God and other people. Was there no end to my learning? What is it next, God, that You want me to do?

15
Fear and Thunder

With my growing understanding of love, the next hurdle was learning how to cope with my fears. I had discovered that love, like the spectrum of light, consists of many colors and that I still had a long way to go to know perfect love. For: "Perfect love casteth out fear" (*see* 1 John 4:18).

Love had done much for me. It had even taught me to accept myself. But I had never been able to overcome my many fears. I feared nearly everything including a fear of fears themselves. Fears had been part of my life as long as I can remember. I had known so many physical threats ever since babyhood.

Thunderstorms were the source of the very first great fears in my memory. Mother was intensely afraid of any *Gewitter* and she had a right to be apprehensive. Our cottage had a straw-thatched roof and was mainly built of wood—brittle lumber of generations past that could burn down within minutes, like a torch. We were too poor to put a lightning rod on top of our house, and the danger of fire was never farther away than the reach of one lighted match or the spark of one electric storm.

Whenever I could hear the faraway growl of an oncoming thunderstorm my stomach would go into knots. Sometimes I wouldn't hear it soon enough because I was a deep sleeper. I would wake up in the heavy darkness of the hayloft where I slept and hear Mother's voice with that edge of fear in it: *"Marichen,* come down. A thunderstorm is near."

I would scurry from under the covers and down the ladder to the main room of the house. Mother never lit the oil lamp when it stormed and thundered; only a candle. The tiny flame would flicker and tremble and form ghostly shadows, the windows would rattle, and the cottage resound as thunderclap after thunderclap would shake the earth. The lightning was always so brilliant that I couldn't shut it out even if I closed my eyes tightly. We would sit and count. As long as there was at least one second between the *Blitz* (lightning) and the *Donner* (thunder) we knew the storm was still not right upon us. Too often the glaring light and the crashing thunder would hit us at the same second. That was always the moment when Mother would say: "Let us pray." We'd kneel down and Mother's labored breath and her thin voice would be drowned out by more crashing and rolling of thunder.

"Protect us, God," she would plead while I shivered. "Send rain to quench any lightning. . . ."

More than once I remember that at just that moment we would hear the sound we had been waiting for so anxiously—the drumming of heavy summer rain as it torrented out of pitch-blackness upon the roof—cooling the heavy atmosphere, wetting the parched earth and lifting the grip of fear from my hurting stomach while I listened with less fright. After a while the storm would roll away as we watched the room stay dark longer between lightning bolts, and the fury of the heavy thunder subsided. I always pictured thunder as coming from a growling animal that was finally driven back by God into his cage where it had to lie down while still grumbling under its breath. Once in a long while we would have more than one thunderstorm in one night. "It's coming back," Mother would call and try to awaken me after I had fallen into a deeper sleep than before to make up for lost nighttime. "Hurry down!"

The animal had slipped out of the cage twice and was trying to get us again, I would think. *Why didn't God keep an eye on the cage door? Was He too busy?*

I conquered my fear of thunderstorms after I had entered school and learned how to read. Books became my friends and open windows to the big wide world I had never seen. Books also taught me about natural science. Thunder became a force of nature in my growing understanding, but I was still afraid. It took a poet to help me over that fear. One day our teacher read to us the description of a thunderstorm as seen by one of my favorite writers of my own homeland. He portrayed the grandeur and power of God in the storm, and the majestic beauty of such magnificent drama. I listened and it left me breathless with a strange excitement.

Yes, I *would* go out into the next thunderstorm and try to see what the poet saw. I didn't have to wait long. I did it the very next day. Luckily, that thunderstorm hit us by day and I could sneak out without Mother noticing it. I stood behind our cottage and watched the heavens turn to fire, and the thunder crashed so violently that I felt the ground shake under my feet. Fear choked me tightly. I couldn't breathe as I watched the fiery fingers of God cut the black clouds into shreds. I dug my head between my shoulders whenever God's voice thundered into my ears. But I didn't close my eyes once and when the rain came I let myself get drenched to the skin.

I stood my ground until the drama was over and the sun peaked again from the west through steel-blue, rolling-away clouds. Then I went into the house and accepted Mother's worried scolding—and thunder never frightened me again. I've been fascinated by it ever since.

Other fears were not so easy to conquer. There was the fear of hail. Today, I know I didn't fear hail itself, I feared the winter following the harvest-destroying hail. It meant less bread and more fights in the house. The less there was to eat, the more my foster-parents fought over me. "She must go," Father would demand. "She will stay," Mother would insist. "I will share my bread with her." I hated myself for eating Mother's bread but I was afraid of hunger. I seemed always to be hungry and would continually beg Mother to give me more bread.

There was a psychological reason for my fear of hunger, but I didn't know this at the time. Today I know. I learned through reading a report of something that happened in postwar Germany. In the American military zone of West Germany were numerous refugee children, often nameless, their ages not known, and with no one to claim them. And they were *hungry.* The Americans "claimed" them. They provided temporary shelters, beds, blankets—and all the food the children could eat! Those hollow-eyed little creatures would stuff themselves until their stomachs would bulge and the nurses didn't dare to give them any more for a while or they might get sicker yet.

In the daytime those kids would be rather content and happy, but nights became a terror for both the children and those who looked after them. The kids would wake up screaming with nightmares, be restless, full of fears, and impossible to quiet down.

An American psychologist was brought in to evaluate the situation and he made a suggestion. The children should be permitted to have all the food they could eat, but before bedtime they were to receive a piece of bread that they were told *not to eat.* They could hold it in their little hands as they went to sleep. For some nights many tense little hands held on tightly to a piece of bread, and as sleepy eyes closed and fingers relaxed, undernourished refugee children learned to sleep in peace through whole nights. But until they had this physical reassurance that they would wake up to more food, fear of hunger would not let them sleep, even though their little tummies bulged with good food.

Countless times I have blessed from my heart this American psychologist (whose name I do not know) for his wisdom. How did he know what to do? Did he, I'll always wonder, know what hunger was like? Had he experienced the fear of hunger, himself? He helped me to understand myself after the war. For fear of hunger haunted me even after I came to America. It was one of the many fears that even the knowledge of God's love could not resolve for many years.

Another fear I had carried since childhood was fear of tension and disharmony. The older I got, the more I learned to bottle up what bothered me. I preferred ulcers to disagreement, and paid with more than surgery for that fear. Whenever communication stops, trouble starts. I had plenty of trouble when my children became teenagers and struck out at both of us. My husband never learned to suspect my pent-up emotions and would be completely aghast whenever I blew my lid.

One of the most acute physical fears I developed after I came to America was my fear of cars. Actually, it wasn't cars I feared, it was accidents. When at last I tried to get to the root of all my fears, I finally came to the conclusion that I wasn't even afraid of accidents —but of suffering. The fear of personal suffering wasn't as haunting as the fear that I might have to watch others suffer or die. It was bad enough to see *anyone* hurt but the thought that I might have to watch my children or my husband get hurt would drive me again and again into near panic.

I was one bundle of fears for many years but nobody, even my own family, knew how deeply tortured I often was. First of all, I had been trained since babyhood to control the showing of my emotions. Next, and more important, I knew how to pray myself through fear attacks.

As traffic would thicken or my husband would speed up (I was too afraid of cars to learn to drive myself, until I became wise and gray) my stomach would begin to hurt and I would pray. I would pray until I had my panic under control and I could act as if nothing had ever bothered me. I was so grateful for the reassurance of prayer, but I often wondered why my prayers never overcame my fears. They made them only bearable. Didn't God promise more than that to His children—or what did He mean in His Word? I found the answer to my own questions while I tried to help someone else.

She was a college student and had come home because she couldn't take the pressure anymore. Raised by elderly grandparents because her parents were divorced, she had been taught right from wrong, and she knew lots of church doctrine and legalism but very little about the love of Christ. We were neighbors and Sylvia and I became fast friends. Nevertheless, she slashed her wrist one night and her grandparents didn't know what to do. I sat at her bedside and waited, and held her bandaged hand. She finally leveled with me while I listened. She was in love with a boy at college. He loved her, too, and they were secretly engaged. They had also gotten too intimate and had gone "all the way." He was a ministerial student.

"Are you pregnant?" I asked her. She shook her head. "Oh, no, I am not," she said and bit her lip, "but I broke off my engagement!"

"Why did you do that; don't you love him anymore?"

"Yes," she cried, "I love him more than ever but I can't marry him now!"

"Why not?"

"Because I believe that God wants me to make a choice. It's either Larry or God. I am afraid of God, so I gave up Larry but I can't live without him, so I want to die!"

"Honey," I said, "do you believe that God loves Larry as much as you do?"

"I don't know," she said, "I want to believe it."

"If you were in God's place," I said, "would you put such a heartache on Larry unless you knew that you wanted to protect him from great harm?"

"No," she said and cried some more, "Larry is so bitter he dropped out of the ministerial course."

"Sylvia, your problem isn't Larry. Your problem is your idea about a revengeful God. Say, 'Yes, God,' when fears strike, and you are free. God will take care of the rest and do what is best for both of you!"

Sylvia struggled for one more week with her fear of losing Larry and finally said yes to God's will. Her fears left, she saw that she had run ahead of the Lord and a year later the two were married. They are a tremendous force for God today, and they have two lovely children.

"Say, 'Yes, God,' when fears strike, Sylvia."—*"Say, 'Yes, God,' when fears strike, Maria,"* I heard the echo in my own heart.

Was that why *I* couldn't overcome *my* fears? Didn't I trust God's love completely? Did I feel that I had to beg and pray and "force" the arm of God my way? If God's love was unconditional, not depending even on human loving response, why couldn't I say *yes* to anything I feared? I knew that nothing could come near me unless it passed God first.

If I panicked because I pictured my children in an accident, I still would have to know that God let it happen because it was for the best. If we could see the end from the beginning, wouldn't we gladly accept God's way for us and our loved ones? I learned to tackle fear after fear by saying *yes* to it, trusting God's perfect love more than my own. I said **yes** and meant it.

"Perfect love casteth out fear" (*see* 1 John 4:18). No human being has perfect love; only God does. Therefore we can paraphrase that text and say: *"God's* love casteth out fear!" Better yet, *our trust in God's perfect love* takes away any fear.

One of the fears I battled hardest with during the last few years was my fear of cancer. I come from a family where, on my mother's side, nearly everyone has died of cancer. I know the odds and I know what pain and suffering can do to me. One of my friends died of cancer a while ago and I nearly panicked again. I was also aware of the fact that our fears often bring on what we fear the most. After a night of struggle, I again said *yes* to my loving Father in heaven.

"God," I said, "if I ever can bring honor to Your name by dying of cancer in the right spirit, may Your will be done!" I meant it. I am not afraid anymore.

By saying, "Yes, God," to every fear that surfaces, I have not only discovered the perfect love of God for my own life in a new depth, I also feel stronger, full of joy, and very free. Fear drains a large part of our emotional energies and paralyzes our acceptable service to God and humanity. Today I know that God suffers with us when we need to suffer hardships because He sees it best for us, but God never suffers more than when we are afraid. Perfect Love (God) cannot help but be hurt in His deepest inner core when we, God's people, distrust that love—and why should we? We can learn to overcome our fear—any fear!

16

The "Germamerican" Gap

Long years before the Americans began to talk so frequently about a youth crisis and a generation gap, we had what could be called the "Germamerican" gap at our house.

It was more than a gap—it became at times a cleft, a rift, and an ocean between the Hirschmann children and their mother. My husband very seldom took an active part in the training of our youngsters. He was gone much of the time and I tried not to make the limited time he spent at home an unpleasant discipline session for the children. It was far from an ideal setup and nothing to be recommended by any means, but we tried to make the best out of difficult circumstances.

Child raising posed no problems the first few years we lived in America. Christel was six and Michael three years old when we arrived. Both obeyed and respected adults, never talked back, and were very easygoing children. Christel could be called a model child. What would I have done without her! She became a second mother to the little Americans who arrived at short intervals. We were a family of seven by the time she became a teenager. I had everything up to that point very much under control and was humbly proud of it. I also had all the answers to successful child rearing, plenty of advice to give, and knew when and how to discipline. *I disciplined intelligently,* I thought, and saw myself as a rather sensible and efficient mother.

That picture changed almost overnight, when my oldest children hit what Americans call teenage time. I wasn't even aware that such an element existed until it was upon me. Later I found out that the word *teen* comes from the Old English word *tēona* which means injury, anger, grief—nothing could better describe those years!

Christel became "Chris" and was actually rather patient with me —at least for a while! She even tried to tolerate my unintelligence due to my Old Country background, and attempted to educate me. She spent agonizing hours, many tears, and much energy in explaining to me that training bras, a shaver for invisible hair on her legs, powder for her youthful complexion, and mascara for her long eyelashes were really not sinful nor a tool of the devil, but plain, basic American necessities of life!

Mike was much less patient with me. He felt insulted to be under the stupid supervision of a German female square who was unqualified to comprehend the superior knowledge of a young American male. I heard one sentence so often that I had a hard time not to scream—and sometimes I did—in response to it.

"Mother," I would hear, "you just don't understand. In America we do things differently. This is not the Old Country!"

The tone of voice was such that anyone could guess that young Americans had superior knowledge in everything, and that the Old Country had brought forth nothing but a bunch of imbeciles of which I was the top one! Mike had had a strong power of persuasion ever since he knew how to use the English language. He, at times, not only managed to convince the three smaller Hirschmanns that their mother was both stupid and crazy, he even made *me* wonder about this!

Oh, the sleepless nights when I would cry silently into my pillow so I wouldn't wake up my husband or anyone else! The desperate prayers for help and wisdom—the endless searching of my soul to understand where I had missed the boat.

Luckily, for the sake of my own sanity and for the betterment of our family relations, the Lord saw fit to send me back to college while Chris and Mike were still in their teens. This didn't change my children, but it changed me. First of all, I got off their backs, at least to a certain degree. Next, I didn't have too much time left to brood over my mistakes. Best of all, it made our family a team.

When a mother of five children goes back to college full-time it brings changes. I'll forever be grateful for the changes it brought us.

I discovered that I had special children, after all: they accepted family responsibilities and stood by me when the going was rough. I found out, too, that I did have a few Old Country problems, as well as having a few good points.

My knowledge of the English language wasn't sufficient at times; I hated history and the Beatles, and I wore "blinders" put on by my different background. Little by little, however, I discovered my prejudices and learned to see broader horizons—for which I shall feel forever indebted to American education.

I am well aware that American education is under fire by its own system and the America of today, but nobody can ever convince me that American education has little of value to offer. I attended several colleges before I finally held that needed degree in my hand. The greatest benefit, however, was not a documented piece of paper but what American education itself did for my own personal growth. It made me a better qualified mother and educator.

I learned to see my own children and the American young people as a whole, in a new light. I had viewed my children as an extension of myself and assumed that they would automatically like what I liked, respect what I respected, and believe what I believed. Young people are individuals, and American young people are *more* so because the entire creed and view of life in the Western culture is geared toward individualism. Our great family gaps occurred when the children caught on to that fact faster than I did. I took it as a personal offense when they liked the Beatles in place of Richard Wagner, whom I had worshiped during my teen years. I also made their own spiritual attitudes my personal responsibility—and that's where I had to learn the most.

Today I know that we parents are very much responsible for our children's religion. Children act, live, and believe what we teach them—until the time when not only their bodies begin to mature and change, but their thinking does, too.

The Jews in Christ's time knew about such changes and a child became "youth" at the age of twelve—it was no accident that Jesus

Christ went to the temple at that age and began to ask questions (*see* Luke 2:42–47). His mind was ready to drop its childlike simplicity and to think in concepts.

Our children think with their senses, tangibly, until they begin to mature. They see love—even God's love—as something visible: a hug, physical protection, a smile, or a candy bar as a reward for good behavior, and they live their parents' religion and faith until their own thinking matures. Teen time is the *first* time a human being watches concepts and theories grow and unfold in the virgin soil of his mind, and it is exciting and frightening. Love becomes more than a hug, and faith more than a distress signal for God to come and rescue him from the bully of the neighborhood. Concepts have a disquieting way of being elusive, nontangible, and vulnerable to doubts; and youth must test and question in order to build their own experimental religion.

It has been said that the more intelligent a child is the more it will experiment and question as a youth. If rebellious experimentation is truly a measurement of intelligence I should be greatly comforted—ours are superintelligent children!

How I wish I might have known then what I know today! Because I had been so horribly misled as a young person, I was determined to protect my own children from such bitter disappointment and I tried to do their thinking for them. It worked so long as they were small; it exploded in my face when they discovered that they were free to think for themselves.

Why do our oldest children have to take in special measure the brunt of our inexperience, anxiety, and religious zealousness? We try too hard, we stuff it down their throats, we scream at them in the name of love—and wonder why they fight back. After all, we figure, it is the simplest, clearest thing in the world to see that they are on the wrong road—haven't we walked the road before and we *know* —why can't they take our word for it?

They can't because they are not made that way and because God has no grandchildren. Each generation must find its own God, its own spiritual concepts, grow its own faith, and have the freedom of choice to test, doubt, question and, if need be, suffer in order to come to its *own* conclusions.

How hard we parents can make it for them! We watch their childlike plant of faith in their primary years and assume that by teenage time it should have grown into a tree. If we could only understand that our teenagers have no real plant to begin with: the first twelve years of their lives put only seeds into their souls. A tiny little plant begins to grow as they learn to think for themselves. Just then we step in and demand more than they can give or produce, even if they try. In the name of a loving Christ we set up unattainable standards, then wonder why our youth give up. They become so discouraged that they let us stamp on their little "faith plant" which just began to sprout, and they sadly leave us to go where they feel accepted.

Too late to undo all the damage I had done with the oldest children: I tried to become less demanding and more understanding with the smaller ones.

Children have a way of soothing our battle wounds at times when we expect it least. Chris got married and all of a sudden I watched her become more conservative than I was at that moment. She had succeeded in modernizing the Old Country model to the extent that she began to be concerned about her Americanized, liberated mother.

Mike continued to test, rebel, and experiment and I learned to carry through with the principles and rules of our home without taking his difference in thinking as a personal insult. I just stood my ground.

I believe more than ever that it is important to teach our youngsters that they must obey the rules of our home as long as we provide food and shelter for them. To obey doesn't always mean that they have to think our way—they have a right to think as they see it best, but they must learn to respect our opinions as much as we do theirs. If they wish to live by their own ideas they must also be willing to accept the consequences of their convictions. Mike did so. He moved out—and matured very fast. The tall, husky teenager who, before he left home, screamed at me, "I hate you, Mother," said only a year later when he came for one of his occasional visits, "Stop worrying about me, Mother. Don't you know better? Have you forgotten what the Bible says?"

"What do you mean," I asked cautiously, wondering how his keen young mind would try to nail me down next.

"Mother," he explained (as though he figured I really *had* forgotten), "the Bible says to train up a child as he should go and he will not depart from it when he is old. [*See* Proverbs 22:6.] Mom, give me time; I am not old yet!"

I tried hard not to cry—Mike detests women who manipulate with tears—and I hid his words in my heart.

I am watching three more teenagers grow into adulthood right now, and I thank the Lord for them. How hard they try to become responsible adults! *"Tēona* time" is a bridge over troubled waters in our modern times; our teens need our love and help. Teenagers don't want to be *always* understood, but their struggles for their own individual identities have to be respected. They need our discipline and consistent rules to feel secure, but freedom of choice to find their own God.

Most of all they need a challenge. There is one American trend I have observed which I simply cannot accept. Ever since America started, Americans seem to have had that urgent idea that they must work and slave and knock themselves out to make it easier for the next generation. America has finally arrived! Young people now have it so easy that they can't stand it. Why? Because youth isn't put together in such a way that they know how to appreciate what comes easy. It makes them restless and they get bored to tears in total security. They don't want their lives prepaid, and their thinking predigested; they don't even want all fun and no hardship. It is a law of life that young people need to test their strength on something greater or tougher than they are. They need a challenge—a cause—and adult models who act consistent and true to their own convictions. Our children are willing to forgive us our mistakes, but if they have any healthy self-respect at all they will not permit us to grow up and experiment for them. They cannot live and learn by our mistakes; they love us most when they have the courage to cut childhood ties and become what God wants them to be: not copies of ourselves, but *God's* own children and mature persons in their own individual right.

It took the period of the "Germamerican" gap to teach me these profound truths.

17

God's Calling

How does God call one into a ministry? That is a question I am very often asked, especially by young people. I don't know how He calls others, I only know how He called me. Since every one of His children is different, I suppose that He has a unique call for every single one of us. But I know that one thing holds true for *any* kind of Christian ministry.

Service for God always begins with an individual experience of finding Jesus Christ. Does that mean that everyone who is in Christian service is born again? That surely would be great, but it isn't so. A person can crusade for an idea before he personally experiences the meaning of it; a human being can give lip service to Christ before he or she knows Him in person. *I* know that better than anyone! I did exactly that. I became a church member years before I became a Christian. I worshiped, attended, gave tithes and offerings, held church offices, and talked about Jesus Christ before I knew Him. Thousands do that today—and thousands wonder why nothing happens in their lives. No doubt, there are some faithful churchgoers who don't expect anything to happen. They like their quiet, secure, uneventful method of "earning their way to heaven." I know how that feels, too! (How does that American proverb go?—"It takes a thief to know a thief." How true that saying is!) It also takes one hypocrite to smell out another hypocrite.

I never found Jesus Christ until I hit bottom in my life. After years of trying to make myself over, trying to forget, trying to improve myself by going to a respectable, fundamentalist church, I finally saw myself for what I was. I looked down and I was covered with filthy rags—my own righteousness, my desperate attempts to improve my misery, my eagerness to impress people with my new humility which I was so proud of!

Jesus and I became friends one warm summer night under the stars before I came to America. We didn't become friends because we were on equal terms; we became friends because I am nothing and He is everything. What a combination that makes! When a human being sees himself in the presence of a holy God, he or she turns into one or more zeros. I qualified for many because I was like Paul, a chief sinner. I had rejected Christ deliberately when I became a Nazi. I despised His name and His life story as unacceptable to German superiority. I saw Him as the mediocre son of an unmarried Jewish girl who conceived Him by a Roman soldier. Then, to cover her embarrassment she made up the virgin-conception tale.

How brazen—how blasphemous—how impertinent we humans dare to be! How smart and strong and capable we see ourselves until we see Christ as He really is. But the more we see Him, the less we become and we add zero to zero, which is of no value. The moment we make Jesus Christ the first and put Him as the great One in front of our zeros, it becomes a combination of value—it becomes a ministry. The lesser we are and the more zeros we add, the greater the value for God.

What a strange formula—but it is God's spiritual law for effective Christian service. If we don't understand and follow that principle we operate with zeros only—and regardless of how many we use, it amounts to nothing: 00000000000000000. . . .

I had no difficulty in seeing my total nothingness when Jesus and I became friends. I was a human wreck and I knew it. My nerves were so shot that I had days when I hardly could tolerate my own family, let alone other people. I would break into tears at the most unexpected times: when someone told a joke, when someone made the least sarcastic remark. I could panic while walking alone on a sidewalk or when I entered a crowded store. My heart would beat so wildly that people could notice it whenever I took part in any discussion or led in small church duties. My ability to handle the pressure of even a normal, everyday life was zero and I knew it.

Will I ever forget how badly my knees shook and my heart fluttered when I was asked to give my first testimony for the Lord? I didn't want to "confess" my past to anyone; I had come to America to forget.

Jesus had other plans. First He gave me small orders. I felt humiliated, I felt shaky and ashamed, but whenever I was asked by anyone, individually or as a group, to testify about my life I would obey, regardless of how I felt.

Even today my heart goes out to anyone who walks up to any pulpit and has that tense, frozen stage fright written all over his or her face. I always whisper a little prayer in my heart for such a person. How well I know how he feels! There was a time when I would literally freeze up like that. My feet and hands would feel like ice and my mind would go blank.

Yes, I knew that I had had the talent of speech while in Nazi school, but when God called me to the pulpit I was afraid and felt as Moses did after forty years in the wilderness. My tongue was heavy with accent and handicapped by a limited vocabulary of the English language; my nerves, tears, and emotions never completely under the discipline of my will; and my body never without pain. Ulcers have a way of hurting at all times, either as hunger pains or as indigestion. Pain or no pain, shaky knees or numb brains—when Jesus tells us to do something, He enables us to do it. He provides what is needed as we set out to obey Him, regardless of how we feel about ourselves or anything else. While we learn to do those seemingly impossible little things for Him, He begins to increase His demands and also the blessings we receive in return.

I would never have dreamed that I would be called into an ever-increasing, ongoing ministry. I expected the public requests to fade out within a short time, and looked at it as a passing phase within my Christian life; a test whereby Jesus was teaching me trust and obedience. After I had learned my lesson I could return to a less complicated, quiet life of ease. It seemed confirmed when I got a telephone call from my doctor one day. We called her Doctor Grace and she had been a true Christian friend of our family for many months.

"Mary," she said, "I can't get you off my mind since you had that last checkup in my office. I think it is only fair that I warn you. It seems obvious to me that you are killing yourself—it might be slowly, but it's surely, my dear! I feel that as your doctor I have a duty toward you and your family. My order is that you stop your public speaking until you are stronger!"

"Are you saying that my public speaking is killing me?"

"Yes," she said resolutely, "it appears to me that your nerves and emotions can never settle down and heal. Whenever you give a testimony about your painful past it is as if you tear open a wound that is about to close, and it can never heal!"

I nodded into the telephone. "I know what you mean, Doctor Grace." I said. "The first few times I gave my testimony it upset me so much I couldn't sleep afterward. It seemed like I was living in a nightmare again for several nights. But. . . ." I hastened to explain, "Doctor Grace, I am better now. I talked to Jesus about it and He took the nightmares away. He is making it bearable, really. Though I relive it every time I tell my life story, by now I can go to sleep afterward. Jesus takes me in His arms. He takes care of me!"

"That might be so," Doctor Grace said, and her voice softened, "but I still feel you should not overtax yourself—give yourself a chance to get stronger before you go on!"

"Thank you, Doctor Grace," I said weakly. "I promise that my family and I will pray about it. If that is what Jesus wants, I shall be glad to do as you say."

I prayed about it and so did my family. The Lord's orders seemed clear: *Go! My grace is sufficient for you. My strength is most strong in the weak* (*see* 2 Corinthians 12:9).

So I went, and went again and again—and again!

Was God's grace sufficient? Yes, indeed! As the years slipped by and brought ever-increasing responsibilities toward my family, my teaching, and my public work for God, I found God's grace not only sufficient but overflowing. It has never been an easy life, but God doesn't promise that for His children. He promises us strength and enables us as we obey His calling, even if it sometimes makes a life of heavy burden.

Christ does not take away our burdens but He carries them with and for us. A person with a "special" calling finds as many—and more—problems at hand as any other child of God. There are family heartaches and family picnics, sicknesses and financial worries, warmth and fireside chats, stubbed toes and warm embraces, misunderstandings and public criticism, sunshine smiles and stormy days; but through it all we have seen God's care and love for all of us. Doctor Grace could be rather proud of me by now: my knees have steadied, my stage fright subsided, my ulcers are gone, and my health has greatly improved. I feel more alive than in my younger years!

Would I do it again if I could live my life all over again? Or would I rather have that quiet, easy life I longed for so badly after I had escaped death, Communism, and my own bitter disillusionments? It was another college student who helped me to find the answer!

A college girl approached me after I had spoken at a youth rally where the Holy Spirit had moved visibly and many young people had accepted Jesus Christ. She was beautiful and very sincere.

"Mrs. Hirschmann," she said, "you must have a beautiful life. You seem to radiate joy and calmness. You don't seem to have any problems. I have often wondered how it would feel to be famous. Your children must adore you. I wish I had a mother like you!"

I smiled back at her. Did I have any problems? They appeared small right after an altar call where more than forty young people gave their lives to Christ.

How does it feel to be famous? Tiresome, living with inconvenience in strange places while home is beckoning; living as a family in a glass house; being watched by many pious ones who are *not* in the ministry but are crusaders of their self-righteousness. Did my children adore me? Sometimes they did, other times they didn't. Glamor and fame stop when daily routine produces frictions, laughter, dirt, and German pancakes.

A beautiful life? *Yes, that I had!* I nodded into her eager face and beamed: "I *do* have a beautiful life, my dear. Anyone does who follows Christ and His calling. There is no other place where you can be happy but where God's will designs you to be. Follow Jesus and He will give you what He gave me—and more!"

18

Inconveniences and Hardships

If there is one fact with which the Christian should reckon it is this: the devil never sleeps.

Anyone who is striving to serve God with the right motive can expect opposition. Those who point to their carefree, untroubled lives as evidence of God's reward for "right living" will do well to look a little deeper. It could be that they're not experiencing the devil's darts because they are spiritually dead. Let them be born again and—watch out! They may find themselves beset by many difficulties.

Should this surprise us? Did not Jesus forewarn us, "In the world you shall have tribulation"? (*See* John 16:33.)

Problems and upsets are often the greatest evidence that we *are* obeying God. We know that Jesus Christ won the victory over death and Satan at the cross. We know that He has all the power, therefore the devil cannot destroy any one of God's children. But, though Satan has no power to destroy us, he, as a defeated enemy, is still permitted to annoy us—and he does.

I still remember the phone call I got one evening while I was trying to do ten things at once, and everything possible had gone wrong. My car wouldn't start. The washing machine had broken down. John had a sore throat. The poodle had run away and the kids were out looking for him while I tried to clean up a house, wash things by hand, and get ready to leave for a weekend appointment.

In the middle of that confusion the phone rang; it was one of my best friends of long years. "I needed to call you for a word of encouragement," Velma said. "I think I must have had the devil personally in my house today—nothing has gone right for me."

"Take heart," I said soberly, "the devil couldn't have been in your house: he hasn't left our place once the whole day. He is working overtime around here.''

After that we laughed and stopped complaining and told each other that actually it wasn't all that bad; no big problems. It was just that we were both fighting the little gnats of life and saw things out of perspective.

I knew better than to do that. God had taught me a long time ago to differentiate between inconveniences and hardships. I knew what hardships were. How foolish of me to let myself get upset by inconveniences. How often we let the devil steal our joy and peace of mind by little annoyances. That is especially true for those of us who are called to preach or teach the Word, I have found.

It took me years to recognize the schemes of the devil and his methods to fight my individual effectiveness for God. During the first years of my public speaking I would simply panic when things wouldn't run smoothly. I would wonder if it was a sign that I wasn't supposed to go, when a tire would go flat at the last minute or my nylons would run just as I got ready to walk on the platform.

It *was* a sign, I learned fast, but not necessarily that I shouldn't go or do as planned. The devil gets very active whenever he is threatened. Veterans in God's service had told me that it is time to rejoice when things seem to go all wrong—it is the surest sign to them that God has something special planned for that occasion.

After a while I learned to look at it the same way—and I learned to give thanks in *all* things: even for late planes and lost connections, for endless airport corridors while dragging all my luggage (I didn't dare to check it since the devil specializes in getting my suitcases in late—if possible, *after* the meetings), for microphones that go out just as I come on to speak, and for hundreds of other problems that beset us too often in this imperfect world.

Giving thanks for inconveniences is not always easy, but, like any other good habit, it can be learned. And it's a sign that we are growing into Christian maturity. It's more difficult to learn to give thanks for *hardships*. This takes a special gift from God—and it is a beautiful gift. I received it as I have any other gift, the hard way, my usual way of getting anything.

As time went on I learned to leave my private life behind whenever I got up to speak for my Lord. I even learned to tune out the worries and heartaches of present and past hardships and see myself wholly as an empty channel to be used by God.

At least I thought I was emptied completely—until I found out that I wasn't! Today I know also that the devil noticed this sooner than I did. Well, hadn't I learned to rise above my embarrassment of being a former Nazi and had tried to take it when my children would be called Nazis in school by prejudiced schoolmates? I hurt for them but I learned to take it. (My children seemed to take it easier than I did.) I also learned to smile when people questioned my motives and called me a Communist. I would take it in stride; I even could discuss it and have a ready answer for anything except that one horrible, dreadful, unbearable truth that I had never been able to face ever since I had heard about it for the first time.

I didn't know that it existed until World War II was over and Nazi Germany had collapsed. The Russians had occupied Czechoslovakia and tried to control everything: our lives, our deaths, our goings and comings, even our thinking. The radio had blared Communist propaganda from early morning to late at night. I never paid attention until one day an announcement caught my ear. It was a Russian report about another of their great deeds: one which accused the Nazi government of unheard-of cruelty.

They gave an eyewitness report about freeing the inmates of a Nazi concentration camp. Thus, the Russians were the great liberators and the Nazis the inhuman brutes. I listened and laughed a bitter laugh. "What will they fabricate next?" I wondered. Nazi Germany was dead, but I still felt like a Nazi. I had no other frame of reference left, no other code of ethics but my Nazi training. Everything else had been brainwashed away. I felt fiercely defensive whenever Nazi Germany was dragged into the dirt. But I had never felt so deeply offended as when I listened to those horrible lies about something they called "concentration camps." I had never even heard the expression before.

"Only Communists can have such beastly imaginations as to fabricate such unbelievable stories," I said to my sister. "The nerve—to accuse superior, intelligent Germans of such atrocities!" It made me recoil.

How little did I know then about the inhumanity of man toward his fellowman. I experienced it myself when I ended up in one of the labor camps set up by the "liberators of Nazi concentration camps." But the misery of my own experience didn't compare to the agony I felt when it finally dawned on me that Nazi concentration camps were not just dirty propaganda, but *truth*—undeniable, cruel, ruthless truth which turned my stomach and made me lie awake at night and feel physically ill whenever I thought about it.

I do not know how other Germans learned to cope with it (and most Germans had the same experience I had. They were unaware, and first heard about those camps after Nazi Germany was no more). I never learned to handle it, not even after I became a Christian and an American citizen.

Even after I learned to "put on the armor of God," the subject of Nazi concentration camps was my most vulnerable point. It was my great skeleton in the closet, the one hardship for which I couldn't give thanks, the one thing I could never face nor discuss. I had to leave it buried in my subconscious to live with it. I had to ignore it in order to function normally. I couldn't talk about it and I couldn't bear to read about it. I felt guilty and innocent, compassionate and resentful, defensive, stunned, aghast—and it stung like salt rubbed into a wound. It was one wound that wouldn't heal and it festered deeper and deeper as the years went by.   .

"God," I would pray, "help me to forget about Nazi concentration camps, help me to bury the past fully. God, You know all about it. I was part of that organization. You *know* how idealistically we were trained and that it would never have dawned on us that such horrors were even possible. I would *never* have given consent to it. God, You know that I didn't know. Why, then, do I feel so guilty about it?"

19

The Nazi and the Jew

Things were going wonderfully well for a change. With my background, this should have put me on the alert. I was on a speaking tour in Florida over Thanksgiving and I was treated like royalty. The television interviews, the news conferences, the social dinners, the speaking engagements—everything was perfect and I walked on clouds. I have never forgotten that I am the orphan girl from the hayloft; wherever people make a big fuss over me, I feel completely overwhelmed and very surprised. But I am human enough to enjoy it and I respond to the American way of showing appreciation. I also feel very much at home with the people of the American news media, and look forward to my various news interviews wherever I speak.

Yes, everything was rosy for me. Until. . . .

I was being interviewed live on a talk show at the largest radio station in the St. Petersburg area. The interviewer, named Art, was one of the nicest fellows I'd ever met. Tall, broad, and outgoing, he acted and looked like a typical, successful American go-getter, and we had a great time. I sensed no tension or trouble whatever. I even forgot that I was on the air live (pretaped programs are easier to do because a poor choice of words can be erased). Art showed so much enthusiasm and know-how about our subject, Nazi Germany, that the time flew by. Our fifteen-minute appointment stretched to an hour. He turned to me. "Maria," he said with a big smile," I hate to let you go. I still have so many questions to ask, would you come back tomorrow for another interview?"

I grinned back at him. "Sure, I'll come back, Art. I enjoyed your talk show very much."

The next day I walked into the studio, all confidence and smiles.

So did Art. "I reserved a whole hour today," he said. "I have a lot of questions to ask."

Still not a shade of possible trouble clouded my horizon, though I wondered how much more he could ask. I thought he had asked all there was to talk about the day before. I soon found out.

Art flipped the microphones on and announced, "I again have Maria Hirschmann as a guest on our talk show. We enjoyed you yesterday, Maria, and our listeners surely appreciated what you had to say about your love for America as you compared your present life with your Nazi past. We had hundreds of telephone calls after the show. However, there is one thing you said that most people find incredible—how could it be possible that you as a high Nazi youth leader *didn't know about concentration camps?*" He underscored the last five words.

I stared into Art's smiling face and bit my lips. My mind went blank and I wondered what to say. I remembered the prior interview. He had asked about those camps and I had answered in one short sentence: "I didn't know about it." That was all. I knew one thing for sure; he had just very politely called me a liar, and we both knew it. I forced myself not to panic and prayed for help.

"Art," I said and cringed, "how can I explain to you and the American people how it was I *didn't* know about it?" I could feel my knuckles tighten to a fist and I knew that my behavior gave every indication of guilt. I took a deep breath. "How would you Americans understand what it is like to live under dictatorship? You take freedom for granted, you always expect to hear both sides of the story —you just don't know how controlled our life was. Really, Art, *I didn't know about it!*" I grasped for more convincing words to say but my mind went blank again.

God knew the truth and so did I, but apparently the American people could not believe me. I didn't know that people in audiences questioned my words, until God brought it to my attention that day. Sometimes the devil has a heyday at our expense and we are not even aware of it.

Art didn't look up. He grunted and I knew he didn't believe me.

That was more than apparent as the interview went on. I sensed disbelief and hostility. It became a cat-and-mouse game. He tried to trap me with questions to admit that I knew, and I tried to prove myself not guilty. It was an unfair game because I was bleeding in my heart and he wasn't. Or was he?

I finally had all I could take, and looked straight into his now unsmiling face. "Art," I said in despair, "would you lay off?"

I caught him by surprise. "What do I lay off?" he frowned.

"Lay off about concentration camps," I said grimly.

"Why?" He sounded puzzled.

"Because you are touching the most sensitive spot of my life! I can't talk about it, Art, it hurts too much. How would you Americans know what it is like to carry a load of collective guilt? I carry it, Art; so does an entire nation across the ocean. Most of us Germans didn't know about it, but we still feel responsible. I was part of a group that killed millions of Jews. I can't even face a Jew today, though I am now a Christian, and Nazi Germany is long gone. . . ."

"Why can't you face Jews today?" Art interrupted me eagerly.

"Because I get that great urge to go up to any Jew and say: 'I didn't know about what happened to your people while I was a Nazi, but I want you to know that I feel so deeply sorry and I hurt so much for you. Will you forgive me?' "

Two big tears formed in Art's eyes and he couldn't speak. It was his turn to talk and I watched him try to answer, but he couldn't. I didn't help him out—after all, he had tortured me long enough.

"What you said touched me deeply," I finally heard him say, and from then on we had the old easiness back for two more hours of interview. I wondered if I would ever get out of that studio! At last he had to close, and he wound up our talk by saying, "Maria, I hate to let you go, and before I tell you and our listeners good-bye, I want you to know something—I am a Jew!"

I felt goose bumps go down my back and I swallowed hard. "I am glad you didn't tell me that earlier," I said and fought for composure. "You could never have interviewed me for three hours with so much ease."

Art walked out. He was his old self again. He smiled and stretched out his big hand. "Maria," he beamed, "if ever you come back to our city, come to our studio. I will put you on even without an appointment. I am your friend."

I shook his hand and thanked him; I couldn't say too much. I was too overwhelmed. *"Dear Lord,"* I prayed, *"does that American boy know what he is doing? Does he know what a gift he had because he grew up in America? Does he know what freedom did for him? He learned to be tolerant, Lord. He learned to be first an American and then a Jew."* I feel that Jews usually carry a greater burden than we Germans do, with our collective guilt. They cannot help but carry collective hate, collective prejudice—but Art didn't! He shook my hand—he was free!

Art was free, but I surely wasn't. I knew I would forever cherish that special moment when a Jew called me his friend, but it didn't ease my burden one bit. "Please, God, don't let it happen again," I prayed. "I can't take it."

The new realization that Americans questioned me added more salt to the wound. It was hard enough to open myself as completely as I did whenever I shared my painful past with them, but it had never dawned on me that anyone would question me. Why would anyone want to tell what I had to tell unless it was the truth, and I had orders from my Lord to do so? I relived it every time I told my story, and I did so to let the people know that Jesus Christ loved me while I was His enemy. (*See* Romans 5:8–10.)

I noticed a new defensiveness in me. I was afraid—and the devil knew it. It had never happened before, but all of a sudden the issue of Nazi concentration camps came up again and again. It was a foolproof method to destroy my joy and throw me into days of depression. One evening I had finished speaking and people crowded me with tears in their eyes and many handshakes. I was jubilant because I had watched many souls accept Christ that night. One man elbowed himself through the crowd, placed himself in front of me and hissed under his breath, "And what do *you* care that six million Jews died!"

If he had choked me with his hands, I couldn't have been more horrified. He turned and walked away before I could answer.

"I do care," I wanted to cry out. "I care so much that I can't talk about it—do you hear me?"

But he didn't hear me and I smiled and shook hands and hurt so badly that I didn't sleep that night as I fought more depression like a black cloud. Then came another talk show in Milwaukee. The day had been filled with TV interviews, newspaper reporters, and other engagements. It was late and I was exhausted. "One more show," I thought, "and I can fall into a bed!"

I walked into the studio. The interviewer looked up without extending a hand. "Hi," he said curtly, "my name is Ira; have a seat."

How frosty can you get? I thought. Maybe I was just oversensitive because I was so tired. I smiled my biggest smile. The man pushed some buttons, shoved a mike into my face and announced his show. He gave the listeners a telephone number they could call to come in over the air. Then he said, "Tonight we have an interesting guest for our show. She is a former Nazi youth leader and her name is Maria Hirschmann. I would like to ask her a question, and please call us if you have any comments about it." Then he turned to me. "Maria," he said deliberately, "did you as a Nazi youth leader know about German concentration camps?"

I forgot to breathe. "Lord," I groaned in my heart, "I asked You not to let it happen again!"

I turned to Ira and looked straight into his dark eyes: "Ira," I said and took a deep breath, "I know what will happen if I answer that question. Nobody will believe me. But I am a Christian and I must tell the truth. I did *not* know about it while I was in Nazi training; I learned about it after World War II!"

What I expected did happen. Within seconds, the light panel that announced incoming calls jammed and remained flooded for two straight hours. For two hours I watched Ira push buttons as faceless voices came in and were aired; and for two hours these American voices crucified and resurrected me on one issue: *Nazi concentration camps.*

For two long hours I tried once in a while to say a few words, while one voice said: "Get her off the air, I recognize her voice; she's a neo-Nazi leader." The next voice came in and said in a German accent: "Leave her alone, she tells the truth; I lived over there, too, and I didn't know it either."

I couldn't believe that it was really happening. I looked at that harsh man, and slowly I watched him change into a warm, concerned human being. As the show went on, Ira, who had brought on the whole conflict by his very first, cold, deliberate question, began to defend me. He defended me more and more.

"Thank You, God," I would pray. I felt I was being judged and didn't know what I had done to deserve all the punishment I was receiving. After two hours Ira ended the torture. He turned the mike off and looked at me. "I am sorry," he said, "that was rough! By the way, I want you to know something: *I am a Jew.*"

I swallowed hard. "Ira," I said shakily, "this *couldn't* happen a second time. . . . I was interviewed by a Jew once before. Let me thank you for defending me."

I stretched my hand out. He hesitated, then he took my hand and said, "I believe you, Maria; the more I thought about it the more I could see that you couldn't have known. You were too confined to have known about it."

"Thank you," I said again and walked out. I felt so drained I could hardly walk. I kept a smile on my face while I dropped into a strange bed and the light was finally out. Then I let my tears roll.

"God," I cried out, "I can't handle it too much longer. You know my heart, You know my emotions. This thing is going to destroy my ministry, my joy, and my walk with You. It's getting too big for me and I have nothing left but fear and guilt. Why, Lord, why do I get crucified? I didn't do anything wrong; You know it! Why are people so cruel?"

20

The Key to Healing

God has promised that He will not let us suffer more than we are able (*see* 1 Corinthians 10:13). Whenever we come to the end of our road and acknowledge it, the Lord makes a path for our feet so we can go on. He made a way of escape from my great emotional crisis in a form I should have least expected.

It was all so very simple—and so great. All true greatness is simple. It seems to be God's way of doing things. We humans love to make things shallow and complicated in order to emphasize our intelligence, but God doesn't operate that way. God's simplicity is very deep, so deep that we can often not even fully comprehend His dealings with us. In one great, simple moment God did not only solve my problem but turned one of my most painful experiences into an overwhelming blessing.

It happened in Dallas at the Christian Booksellers' convention. My *Hansi* book was to be introduced to the American public for the first time and I spent three days at my publisher's booth autographing my new book. I hadn't seen the jacket of the book until I arrived in Dallas. I cringed when I saw the big swastika right above my name. "Did they *have* to do that?" I groaned. My publisher must have thought so. And I had to admit it did capture attention.

There seemed to be a big interest in that book right from the beginning, and I autographed, shook hands, smiled, visited—and walked on clouds. The air around me crackled with spiritual excitement and I wondered what heaven will be like someday when Christians on earth can have such joy feasts as we had in Dallas.

People were so good to me, in spite of the big swastika on my book cover, and nobody asked me any embarrassing questions or made any disturbing remarks. That is, until the last day of my stay. My editor, Virginia, turned to me and said, "Hansi [by then everybody had begun to call me Hansi] do you know who is speaking at the luncheon today?"

"No, I don't," I smiled at her. I felt all excited inside because the daily luncheon was the great highlight of every day and I had enjoyed the previous two luncheons to the fullest. "Who is speaking this noon?" I asked eagerly.

"Corrie ten Boom."

I looked blank. Virginia said no more.

"Who is she?" I asked innocently. My editor eyed me over her glasses.

"She is the author of *The Hiding Place;* she is. . . ."

"Isn't that the book about a concentration camp?" I interrupted her.

"Yes, it's a great best-seller—haven't you read it?"

I just said *no* and walked away. I wondered what Virginia thought about my strange behavior but I had no choice at that moment. I had to get away and get over my inner fright. I couldn't answer any more questions and I had to give myself some stern advice.

It was stupid, childish, and hysterical to fall apart about such a thing, and I knew it. I could reason it all out, analyze it as a psychologist and try to apply common sense and my will—but I couldn't stop my stomach from going into knots and the lump in my throat wouldn't go away. It got bigger while I ate and visited—and waited. I kept my eyes on the platform. Finally a pleasingly plump, elderly lady made her way to the microphone. I watched her walk very slowly and deliberately (I found out later that she was eighty-two years old that summer) and I watched more than two thousand delegates stand up and give that lady a standing ovation before she had said her first word.

I stood up with the others and wondered: *Who is that woman? What makes her so special?*

I soon found out. Corrie ten Boom began to talk—she never preaches—and Corrie ten Boom talks with more than her words. Every movement of her hands, every expression of her face, and the language of her body speaks as loud or louder than her tongue—and all of it has *one* message: **love.**

Corrie ten Boom oozes love! She did so that noon, and I listened—and I relaxed. I couldn't help it and I didn't want to, either, it was too beautiful! I soaked it all in and thanked God for that message until I heard her say three words: *German concentration camp!* She began to describe the bitter sufferings, told about her sister Betsie's death, her own experience of walking through that gate back to life instead of going to the gas chamber, as all the other women of her age group did. I felt an overwhelming desire to get up and walk out. I ached so badly and my heart screamed within me. "My God," I cried silently, "it is true, it is all as terribly true as I have heard it described before. That woman is a Christian and she wouldn't lie! God, how can I carry the thought that a woman like her was treated so horribly by the group I belonged to?"

Corrie talked on and I listened. She told how she got back to Holland and World War II was finally over. Corrie's starved, swollen body recovered and she remembered her sister Betsie's words just before she died: "Corrie, we must help those people after the war is over. We must show them that love is greater. . . ."

"God," Corrie ten Boom prayed, "I am ready to go and help people. I will tell about Your love and that it is greater than hate. Where do You want me to go, Jesus?"

"I want you to go to Germany," the Lord said.

"I'll go anywhere, but I don't feel I can go back to Germany," Corrie pleaded.

"Corrie, you must obey or My Spirit will not be in you—I will not talk to you anymore!"

Corrie argued, cried, prayed and—longing for Christ's presence in her heart too much to disobey His command—she went to Germany. The German people flocked to Corrie and to Corrie's God. They learned to love Him by loving her.

I felt tears sting my eyes. *How could they help it,* I thought, *how could anybody help but love her?* Corrie talked on in her accented, warm voice. She told how she spoke in a church in Munich one day in 1947.

Yes, she told those defeated Germans about God's love and forgiveness. Solemn faces would stare at her, not quite daring to believe. They left, moved, in stunned silence after the meeting and then she watched a man working his way down the aisle toward her.

He wore an overcoat and a brown hat but she had seen that face before, under a visored SS cap with its skull and crossbones. He had worn a blue uniform and she remembered his swinging leather belt. He had been one of the most cruel guards and Betsie had suffered at his hands—and died!

The man stretched out his hand: "I was a guard in Ravensbruck," he said, "I know that God has forgiven me for the cruel things I did there—will you forgive me, too?"

Corrie related to us that she stood there and thought: *I cannot forgive! Oh, Betsie, can he erase your slow terrible death simply by asking for forgiveness?*

Then, raising her arm, she pleaded, "Jesus, help me—do what I cannot do." And woodenly, mechanically, she thrust her hand into the hand of the former guard—and a healing warmth flooded through her toward that man.

"I forgive you, brother," Corrie cried, "I forgive you with all my heart."

Corrie ended her talk by quoting a Bible text, but I was sobbing too hard by then to grasp her final words. I had to get up and walk out. I tried to get hold of myself in the ladies' room; I washed my tear-stained face and walked back to the booth to autograph more books. I smiled, visited, shook hands, and my heart cried. "Lord," I pleaded over and over, "let me meet Corrie ten Boom before I go home!" (It was my last afternoon at the convention.)

Would I have a chance? People crowded me and, anyway, I was not so sure I'd even have the courage to go and find her. I did, after the afternoon crowd had gone away and the booth was empty. I grabbed an autographed book and made my way quickly down some aisles before I could change my mind. My heart sank when I finally found her. People stood in a long line waiting to meet her and to receive an autographed copy of her book. I squeezed through the line of people and found her secretary.

"I am a fellow author. May I speak to Corrie ten Boom for just a moment?"

The blond young woman smiled at me. "Of course, go right ahead," she said. Her accent was so cute!

Corrie sat in a low chair and people filed by. They talked, hugged her, and took what seemed to me endless minutes to visit with her. I took a deep, shaky breath and knelt down beside her chair. I hid my book behind my back.

"Corrie," I said, very tense as I felt my courage ebb away, "I am a fellow author and I wanted to give you my book. Would you be willing to read it? I am from the other side."

Corrie's innocent, childlike face turned toward me. She smiled, "What other side?" I brought the book from behind me and held it before her eyes.

"This side," I said and watched her face closely.

She looked at it—the swastika, the title, my name—and I held my breath and watched for even the smallest flicker of resentment in her kind eyes. I knew I would turn and walk away if there was even the slightest sign of pain in her face, but there was none.

There was only love: warm, compassionate, Christlike love, and a smile and many precious wrinkles. Then she spoke in the language that must bring a thousand horrible memories to her—she asked me softly in German, *"Von wo bist du?* [From where are you, my dear?]" The *du* (you) form is only used for friends and family in the German language; strangers are addressed by the formal *Sie* (you or they).

To me, *The Girl Who Loved the Swastika,* as the jacket of my book proclaimed, Corrie ten Boom said, *"Von wo bist **du?**"*

My eyes filled with tears. I swallowed and said, "I am from Czechoslovakia, but my mother tongue is German. I was trained in a Nazi school, but I found Jesus after World War II, and we came to America. I wrote a book about it. Would you be willing to read it?"

Corrie's smile got bigger. "So you are *Hansi?* Of course I shall read your book!"

"I autographed it for you," I said and gave it to her.

"Thank you," she said ever so graciously, "now let me autograph one of my books for you!"

She didn't give me her most famous book *The Hiding Place;* she picked up her little book *Amazing Love.* In it she wrote in German: *"Für Maria Anne von Corrie ten Boom."* Under it she wrote in English: "An ocean of love is available. Romans 5:5." She handed me the book. I kissed her wrinkled cheek and wiped my tears away. I stood up and walked away with her book in my hand and I felt like singing.

Did my feet touch the ground? They must have! I got back to my publisher's booth and joy seemed to lift me off the ground. I felt so light, so free, so emptied out—the skeleton in my soul was gone and I knew it.

"God," I said, "I am free at last, I am all whole inside. I am healed! Thank You God, oh, thank You so very much!"

Healed at last—and free enough to go and buy *The Hiding Place* as soon as I arrived home the following day! I read that book. It will never be an easy matter for me to read such books. I sobbed myself through the last half of *The Hiding Place.* Several times I had to stop and just let the tears run freely before I could go back to it, but I finally got through the book. When I laid it down, I couldn't see too well through tear-dimmed eyes, but my soul had a new vision of Christ's love.

I sat down and wrote Corrie ten Boom a letter. I didn't know if it would reach her; I didn't even think she would answer me. I just obeyed my great urge to say, "Thank you," and tell her what she had done for me. Of course, Corrie ten Boom did answer me; she did more than that—she called me to her side!

"Hansi," she said, "come and see me! I loved your book and I love you. I want to see you again!"

She is my *Tante* (Aunt) *Corrie* since we embraced each other that happy afternoon when we met again—and again—and again—and

I am "her Hansi" and I cherish every moment we can have with each other.

We don't see each other too often. We are both going about our Father's business. Both of us have a calling, both of us have a message from God. The urgency of that message becomes greater and deeper as we watch America turn away from her great Christian heritage to materialism, intellectualism, and hate. We watch Americans cling to their freedom but separate themselves from the inner control of the love of God. Freedom without God is doomed to die: it becomes lawlessness and leads to annihilation. Corrie and I were once on opposite sides but we both learned the same truth: Whenever people disobey the great God who gave the concepts of love and freedom of choice to every individual, the people pay a horrible price. "Where there is no vision, the people perish" (*see* Proverbs 29:18).

America will not come to an end because it had a Civil War or a Watergate scandal; America will stop being a nation under God and a free democracy when the American people forget what has made their nation great. It is their Christian heritage. Love and forgiveness (the essence of Christianity) have been part of American history from its beginning. Every crisis in the past and every deep rift was mended because someone reminded and warned the American people, in time, that they must forgive and rebuild and have faith in God.

I shall never forget what Corrie ten Boom said to me the last time I saw her. I told her I had resigned my teaching job and was now giving full time to my lecturing and writing. She looked pleased and nodded. "Good, my dear Hansi," she said, "and don't forget that the most important message we have for the American people at the present is that God is asking them to forgive one another."

"I know," I said, and felt deeply moved. "God has shown me the same thing. I have watched America being torn apart by the intensity of the Watergate scandal—and it frightens me. It's almost as if Nazi Germany was rearing its ugly head again. And, *Tante Corrie,*" I confided to her, "I heard God giving me clear orders; it was one night when I had prayed and fasted before Him, and God spoke to me."

*Go and tell the American people that they need to be healed.
And I, the God of their fathers, will heal them. But the key
to healing is forgiveness.*

Corrie nodded in agreement. "Yes, people must forgive *with their
will,"* she declared. "That is man's part and the first step. God's Spirit
will do the rest and heal everything that hurts, *even our memories!"*

What a wonderful God we both serve! His love is so simple and
so great. All it takes from our side is a willing, "I forgive you." These
three words will not only open the door of healing into our own lives,
but they can make America again "a nation under God." America
is yet a land of individuals who are still free to make their own
choices.

Our willingness to forgive must not depend on the other person's
readiness to repent or confess. Whenever we forgive, we shall heal.
Whenever we love, we are free. *What a great choice we all have.*
I am not afraid anymore of what the future might bring. All I ask of
God is that I might never become unfree again. He may purge me
with suffering if I need it; He may wash my eyes with tears if I lose
my vision. As long as He makes me willing to be made willing to
forgive, I can take any hurt that lies ahead of me. I shall give thanks
to Him for all things, and praise Him.

Hasn't God been good to me?
Once I was blind, and now I can see—***through HIS eyes!***